*CREATED
FOR THE
UNDEFINED.*

CONTENTS

MAY 2020
ISSUE 02

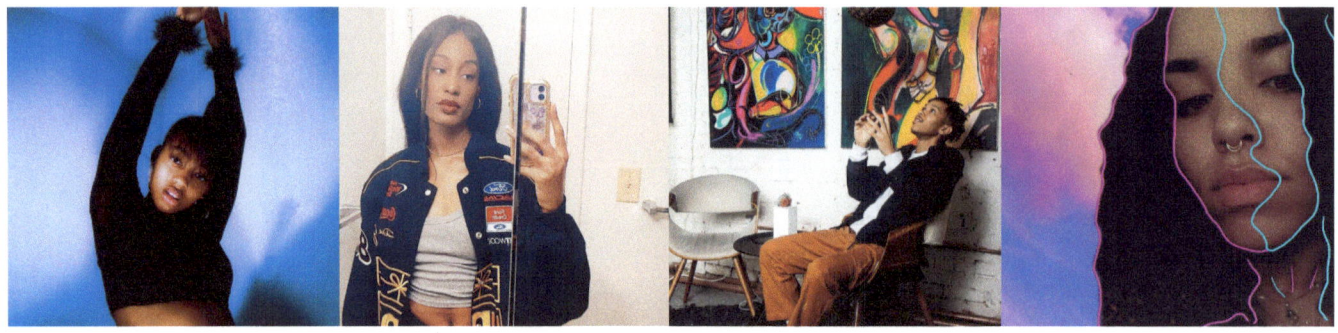

07 ARIAL ROBINSON

11 JESIAH ATKINSON

15 RAIN SPANN

19 GABRIELLE BELMER

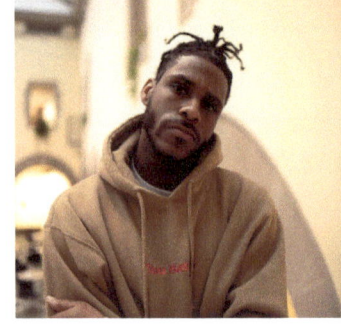
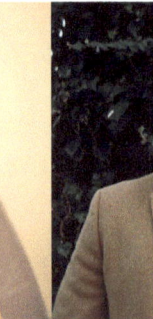
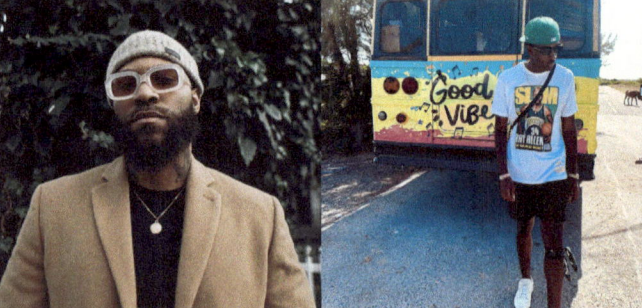
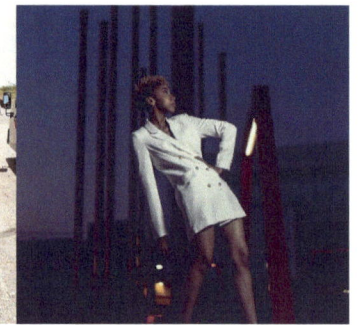

23 DAIQUAN DAVIS

26 CHRISTOPHER HALEY

30 CAMERON LIDE & KERISSA NEWMAN

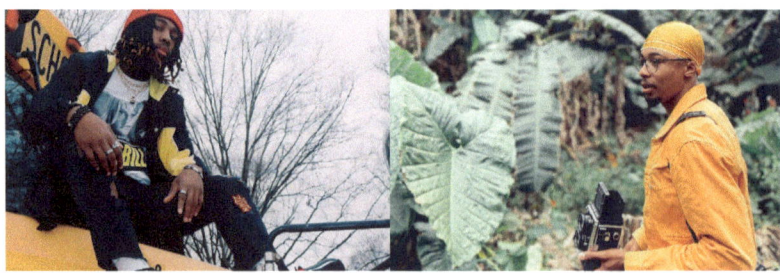

34 JORDAN POPE

38 "30"

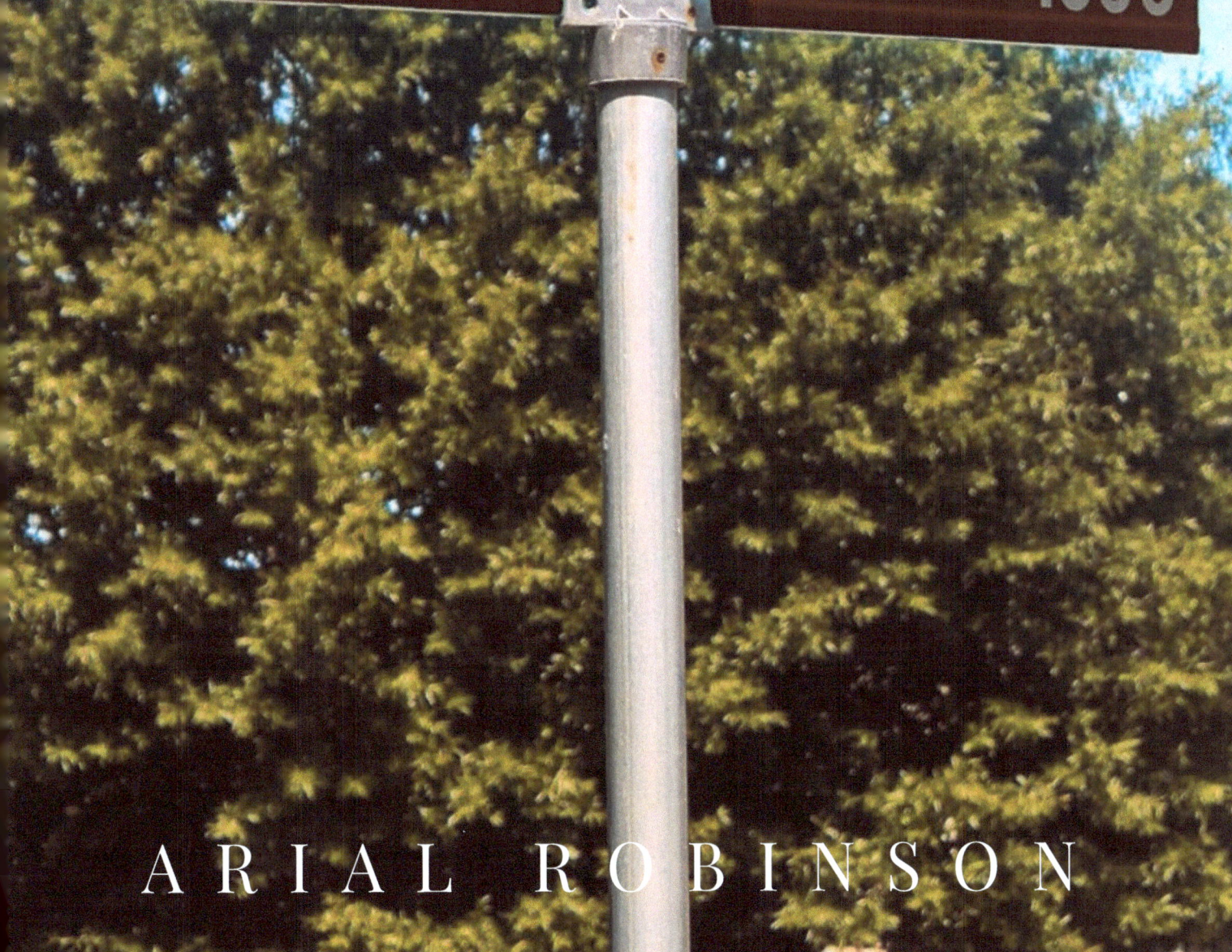

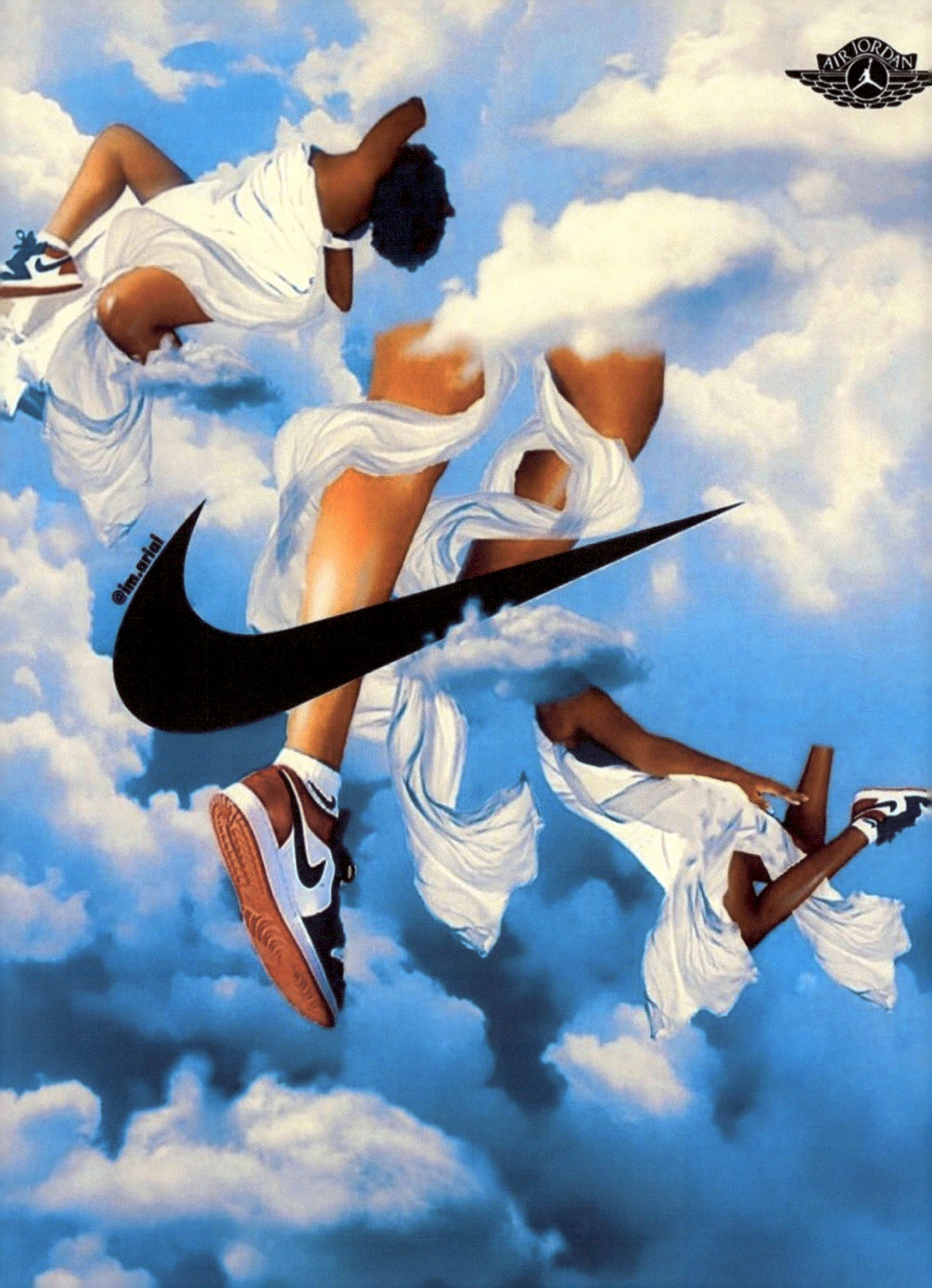

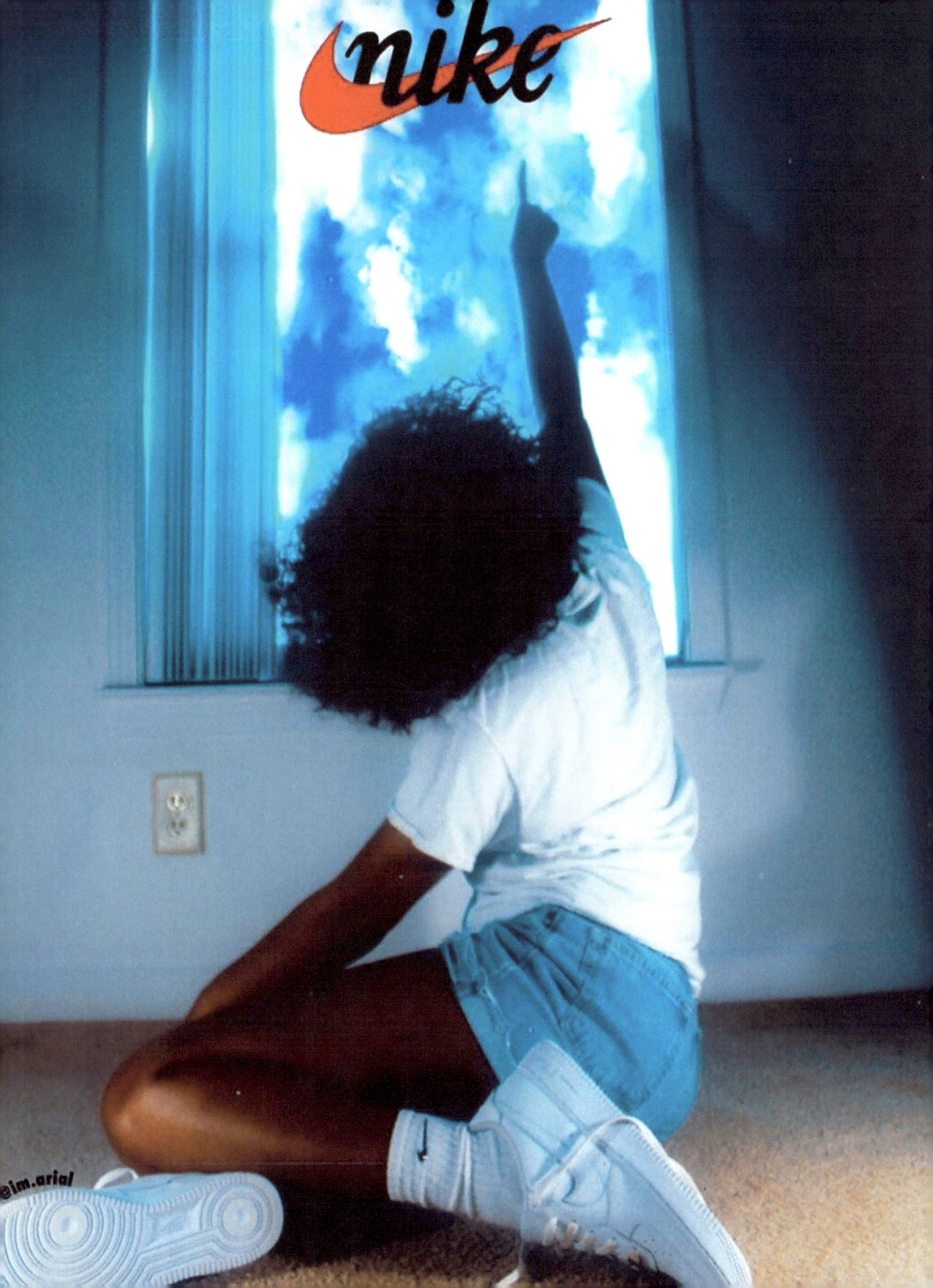

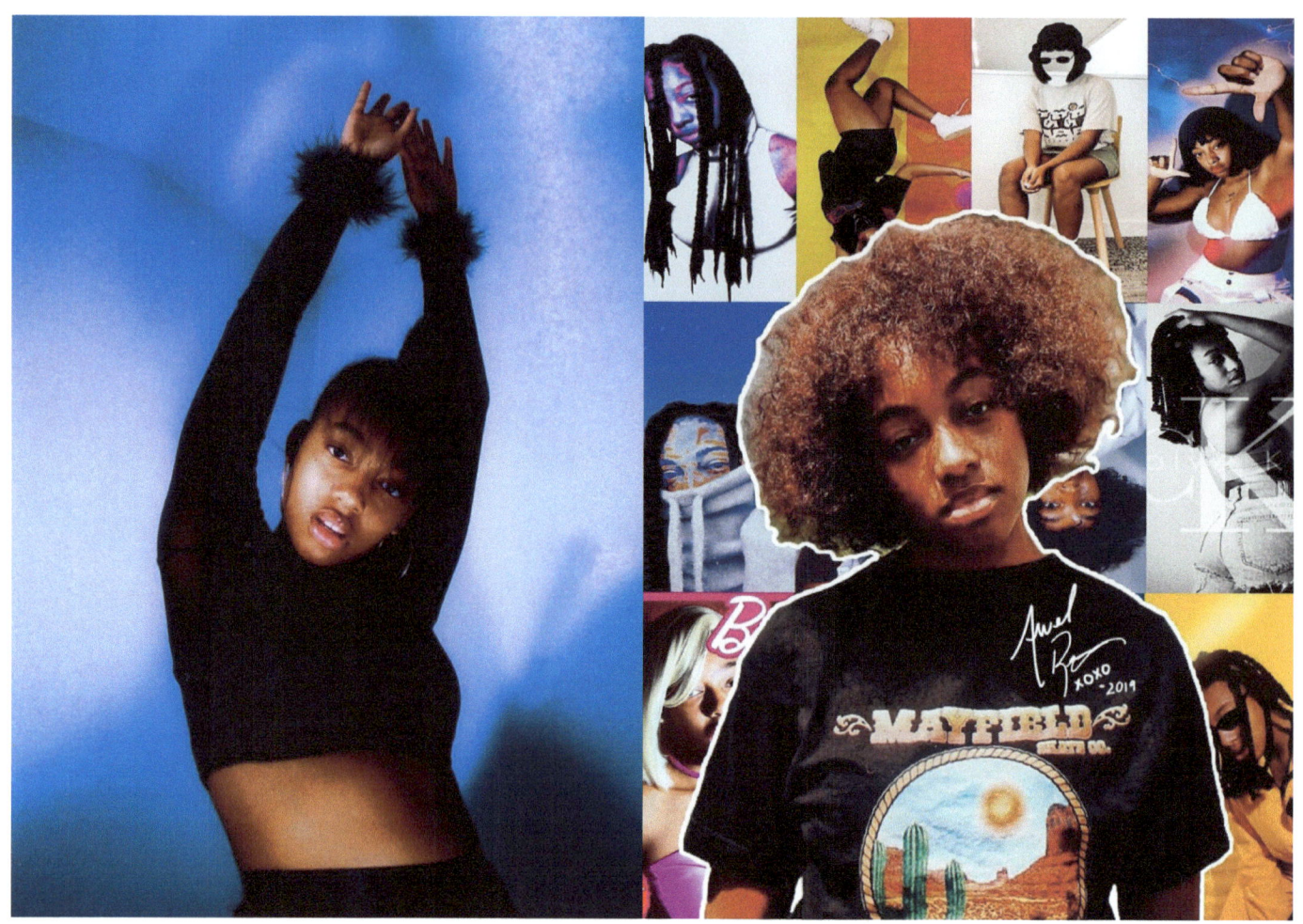

ARIAL ROBINSON

LIMITLESS CREATIVE

Drawing inspiration from creative's like Tyler The Creator, Sean Brown, Beyonce & Steve Lacy, Arial knows not to let the world tell her what she can and can't be. Her range as a creative certainly stands out, with her projects ranging from photo shoots, to an entire clothing collection. However, one of her best projects to date is her very own published book, The Modern Day Black Alphabet. Her book not only consists all 26 letters, but each letter has a picture that describes each of them perfectly.

With Arial's artistic expertise, she'll have no issues achieving her goals of working with brands like Nike and New Era. As well as collaborating with schools and educators across the nation that will help spread her book to the under served communities that lack proper avocations and representation.

"I DON'T HAVE ONE BIG INFLUENCE, BUT I DO LOOK UP TO MY MOM, BECAUSE SHE'S VERY HARDWORKING AND RESILIENT."

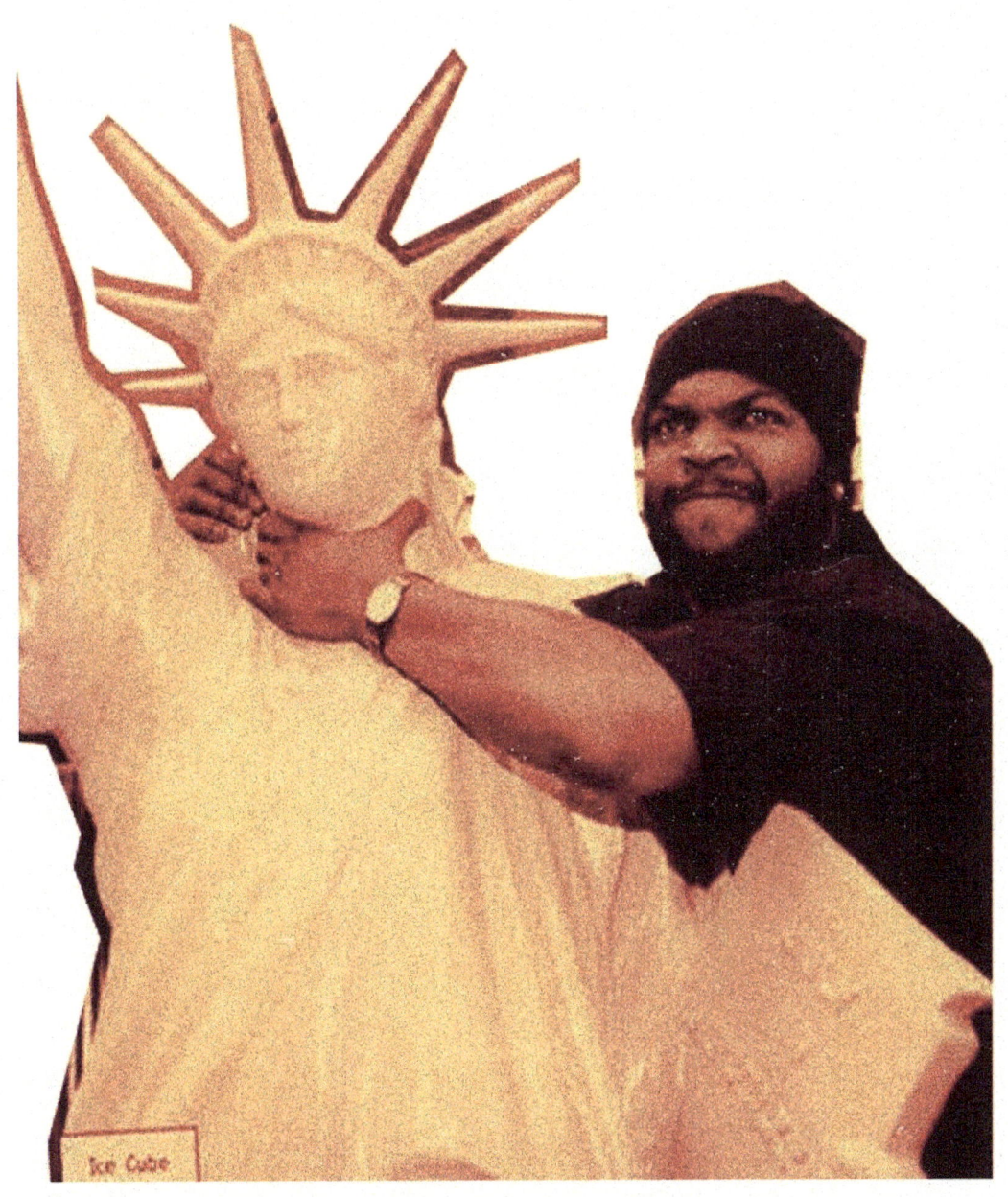

SUGAR
TELEVISION

DOLBY DIGITAL

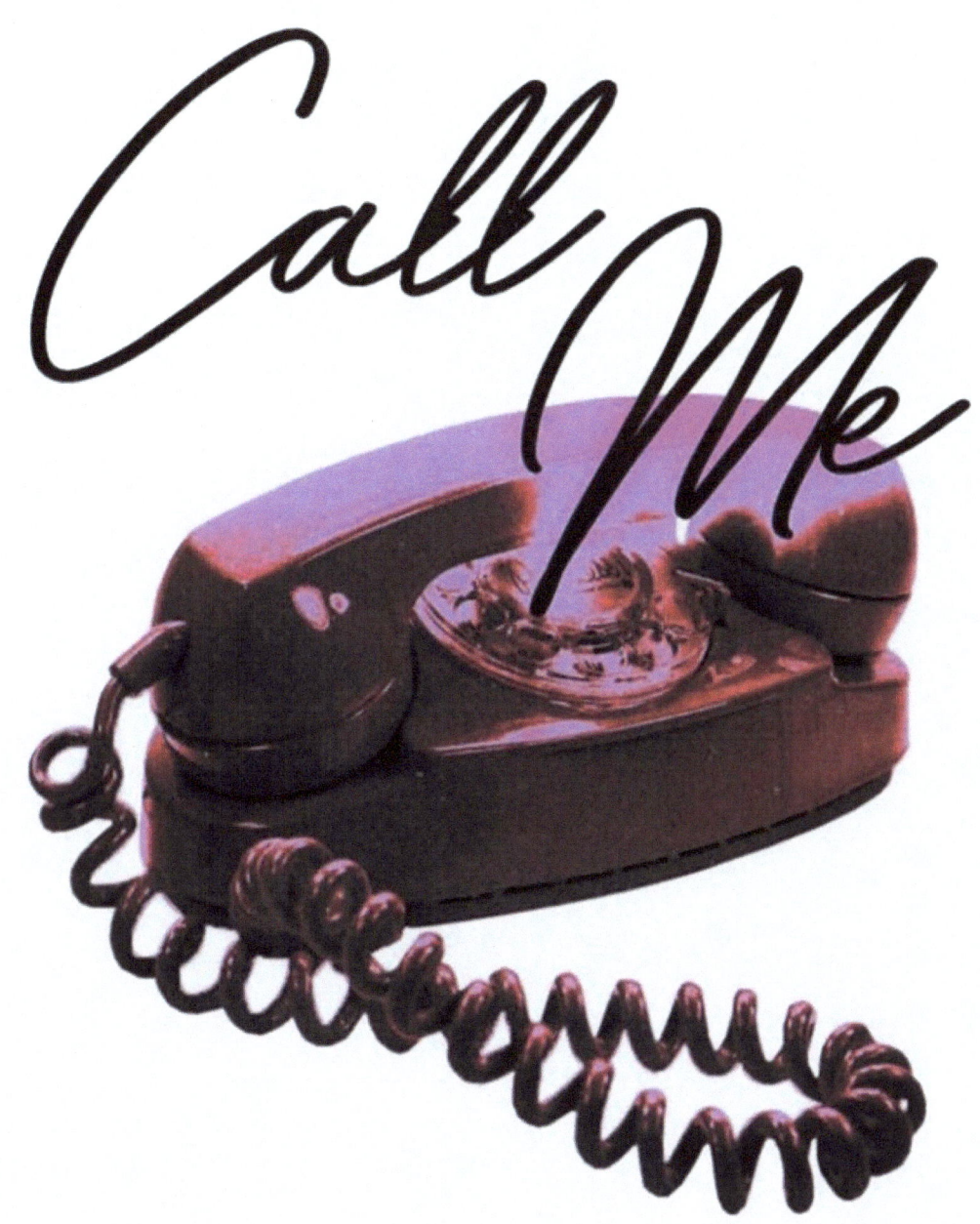

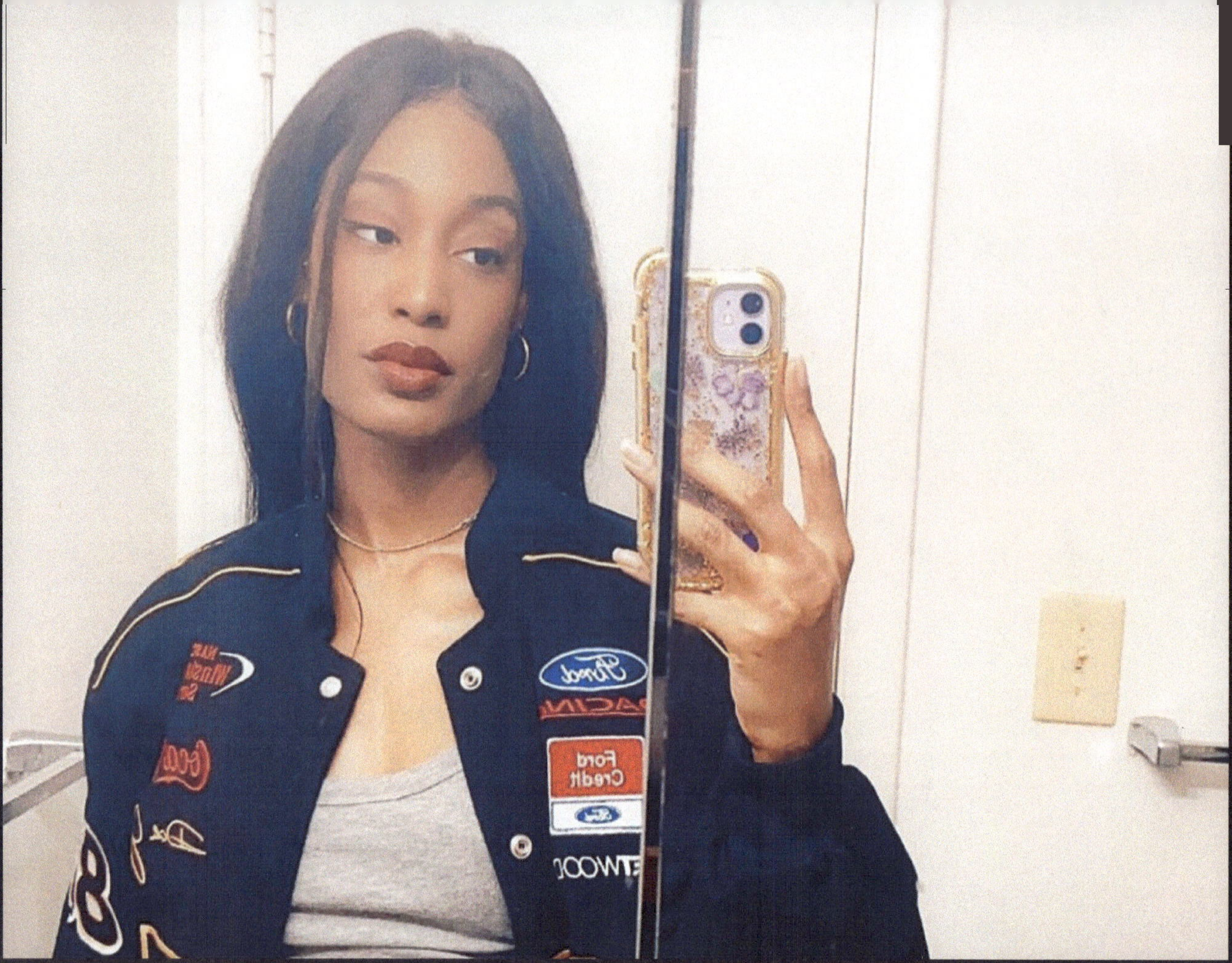

JESIAH ATKINSON

WORLD RENOWN DESIGNER

One of the best designers we have seen, Jesiah has seriously turned heads with her work. One of her best collections being the "365 Challenge," where she creates fresh designs everyday of the year has been illustrious. From the day she started, July 19, 2019, to present, her work has seriously improved. Miraculously, this challenge has opened many doors for her, like working with celebrities such as, Caleon Fox & Kim Petras.

Her potential is limitless and she's only getting started. When asked where she draws her inspiration from, she stated, "I'm more inspired by time periods rather than people most of the time. The 70's-90's was a golden age for design." Jesiah is confident that her skillset will take her places she would've never imagined.

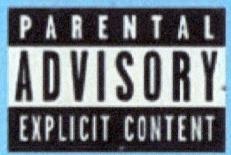

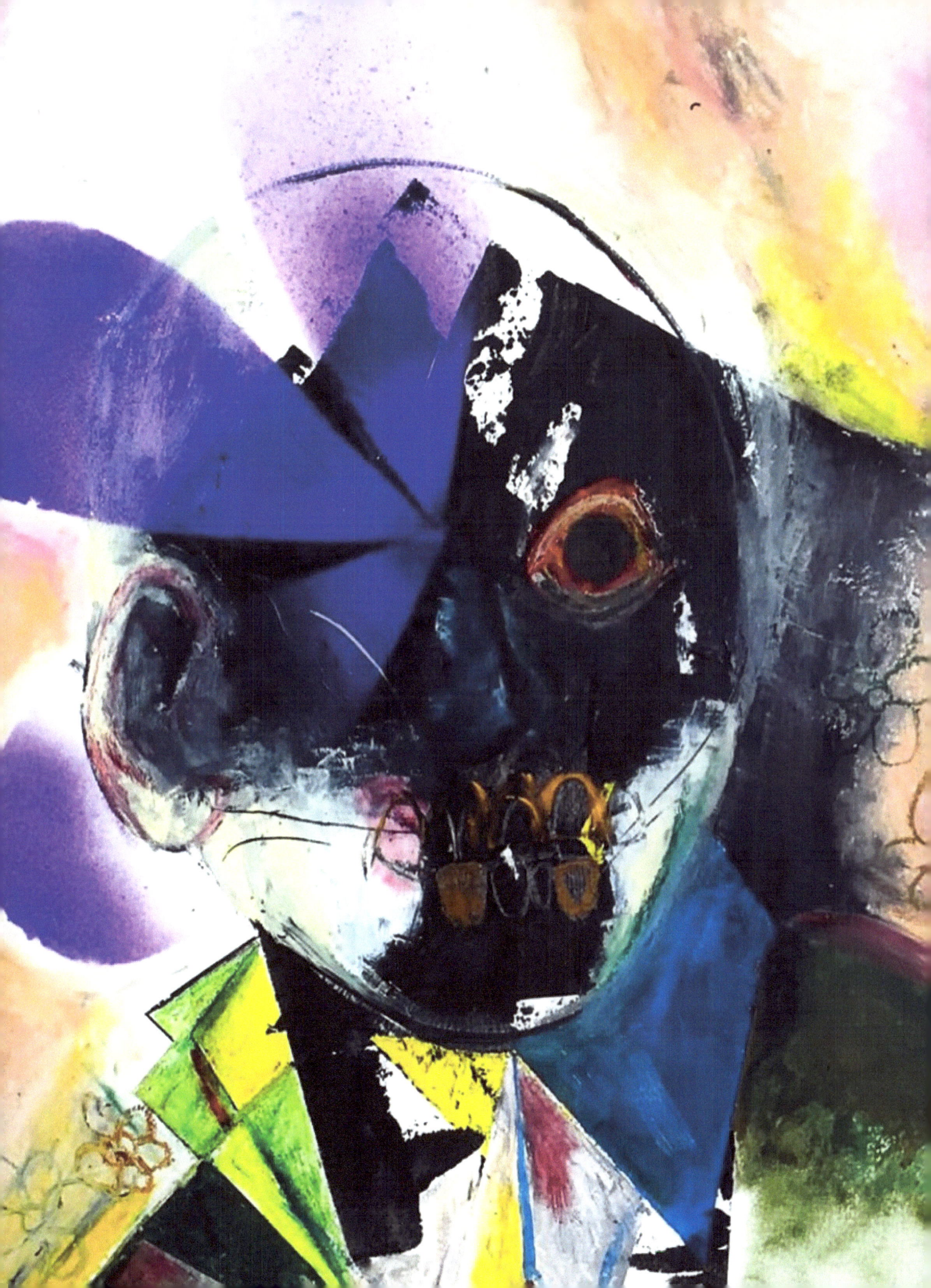

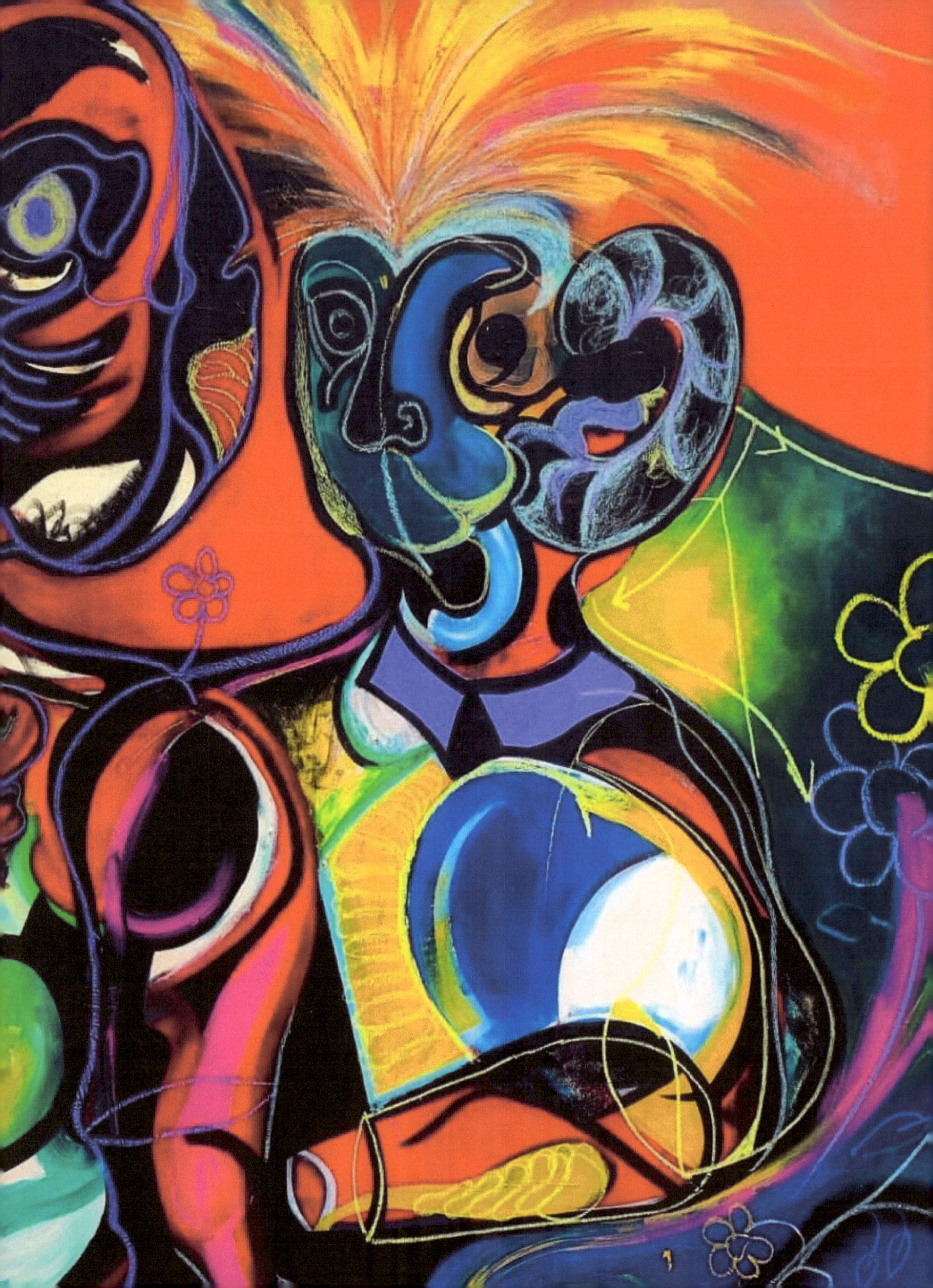

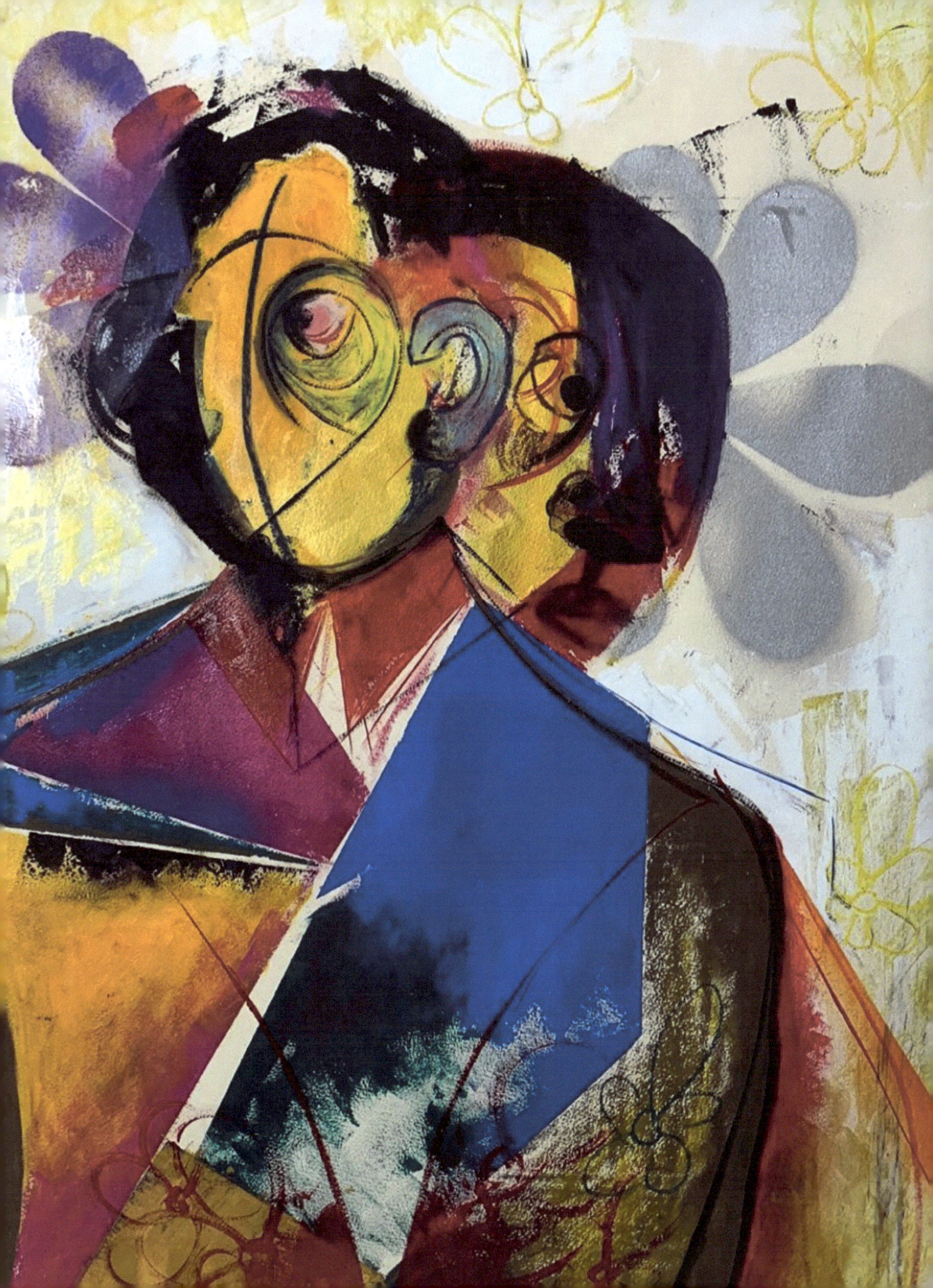

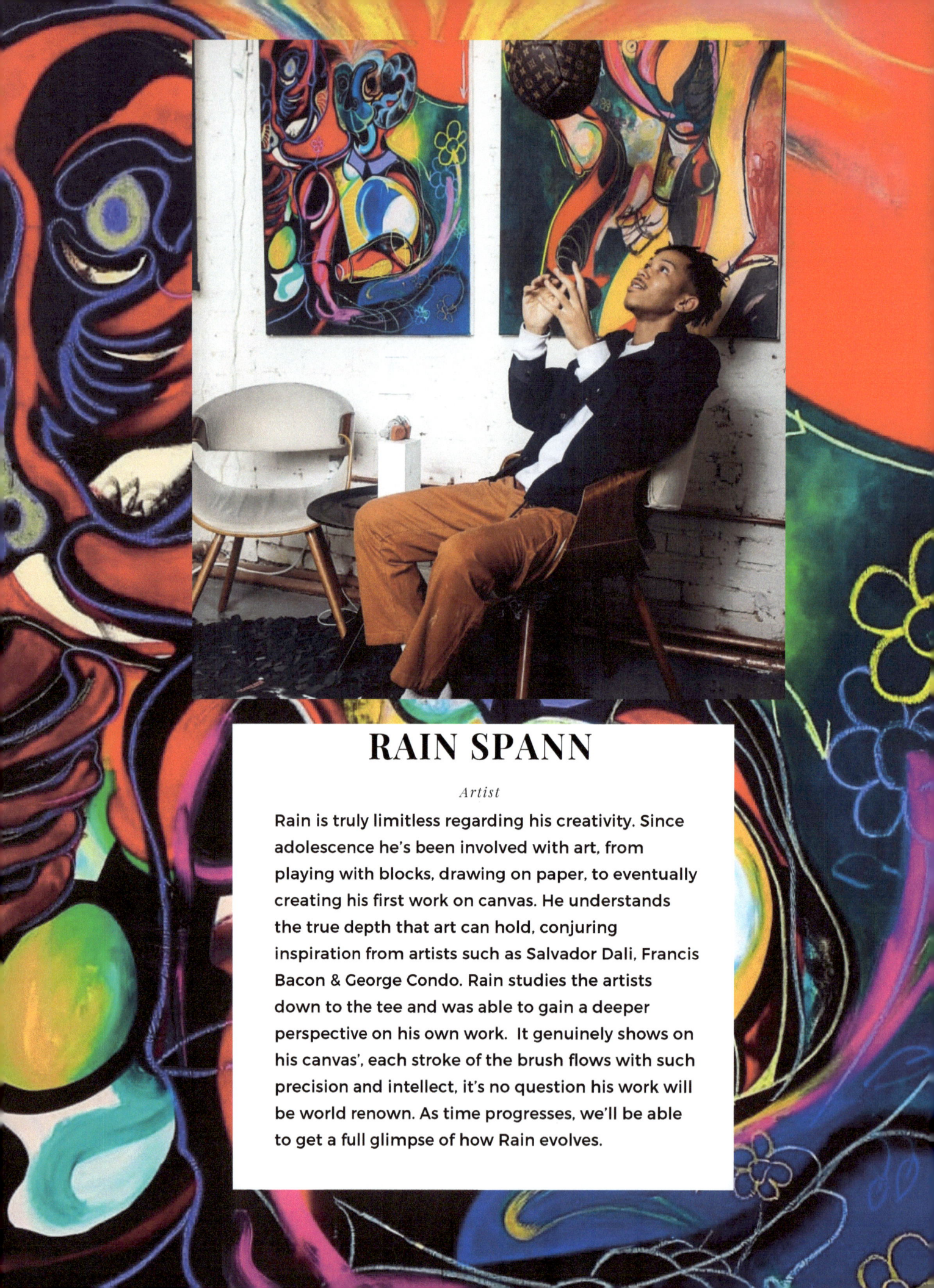

RAIN SPANN

Artist

Rain is truly limitless regarding his creativity. Since adolescence he's been involved with art, from playing with blocks, drawing on paper, to eventually creating his first work on canvas. He understands the true depth that art can hold, conjuring inspiration from artists such as Salvador Dali, Francis Bacon & George Condo. Rain studies the artists down to the tee and was able to gain a deeper perspective on his own work. It genuinely shows on his canvas', each stroke of the brush flows with such precision and intellect, it's no question his work will be world renown. As time progresses, we'll be able to get a full glimpse of how Rain evolves.

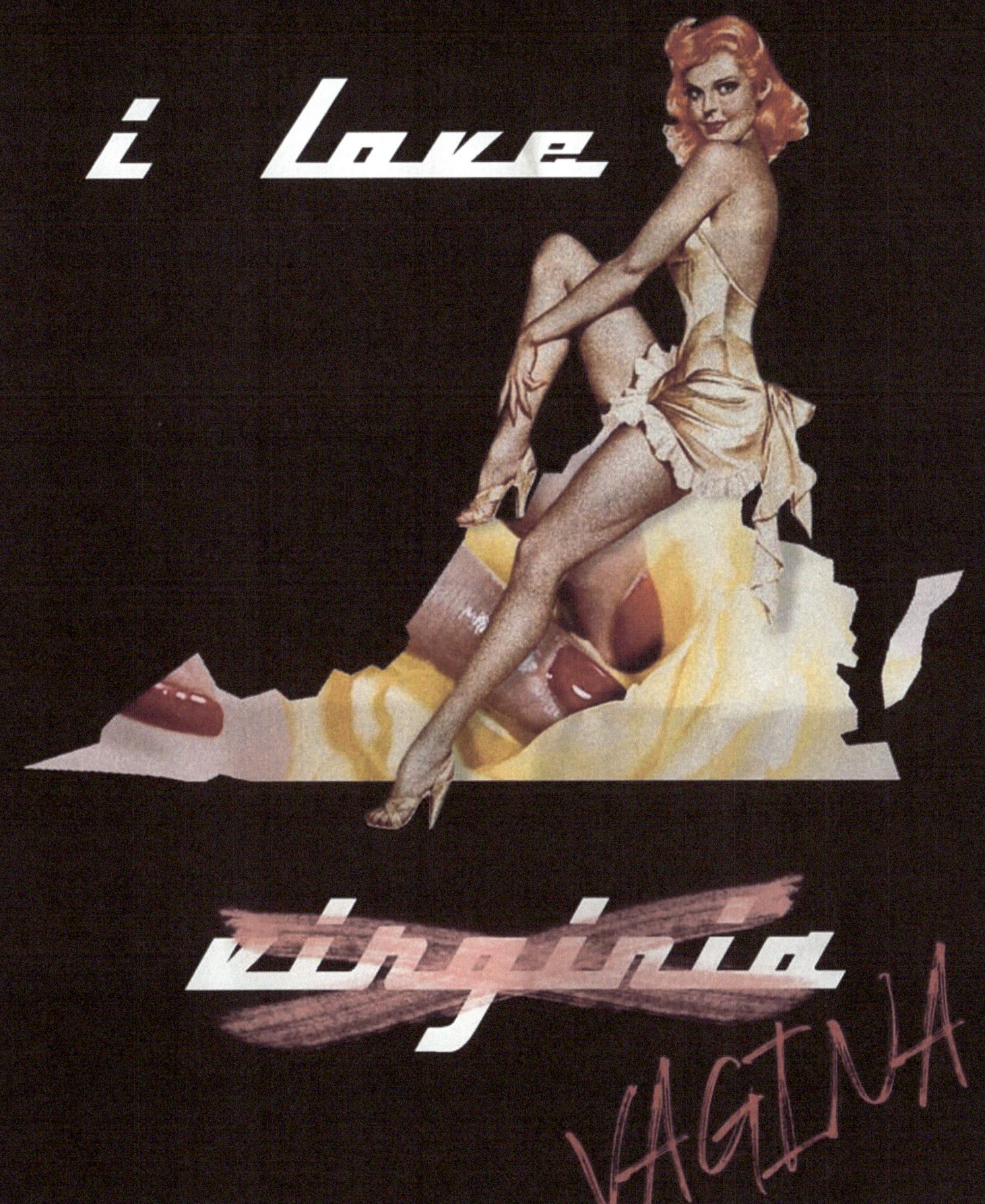

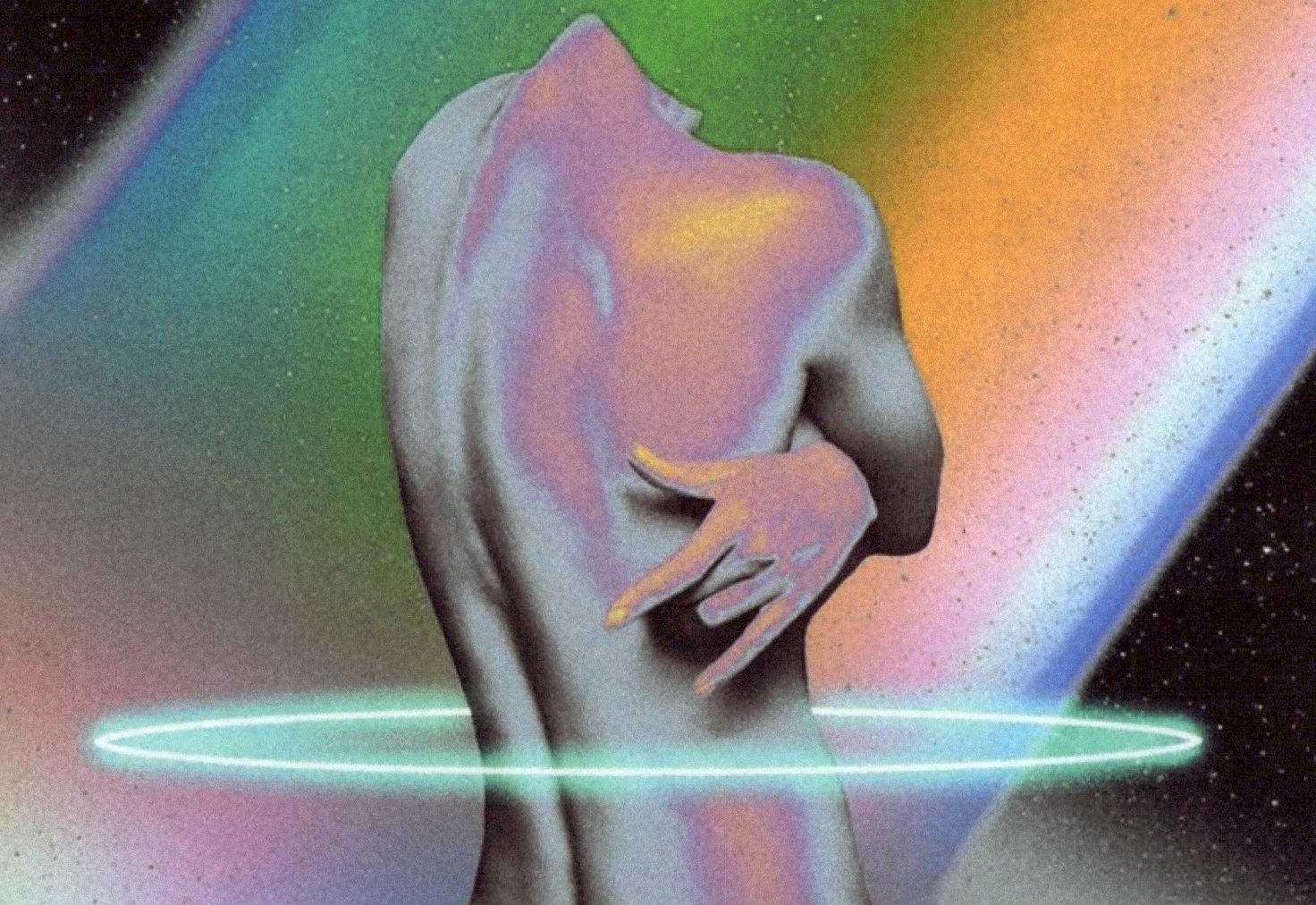

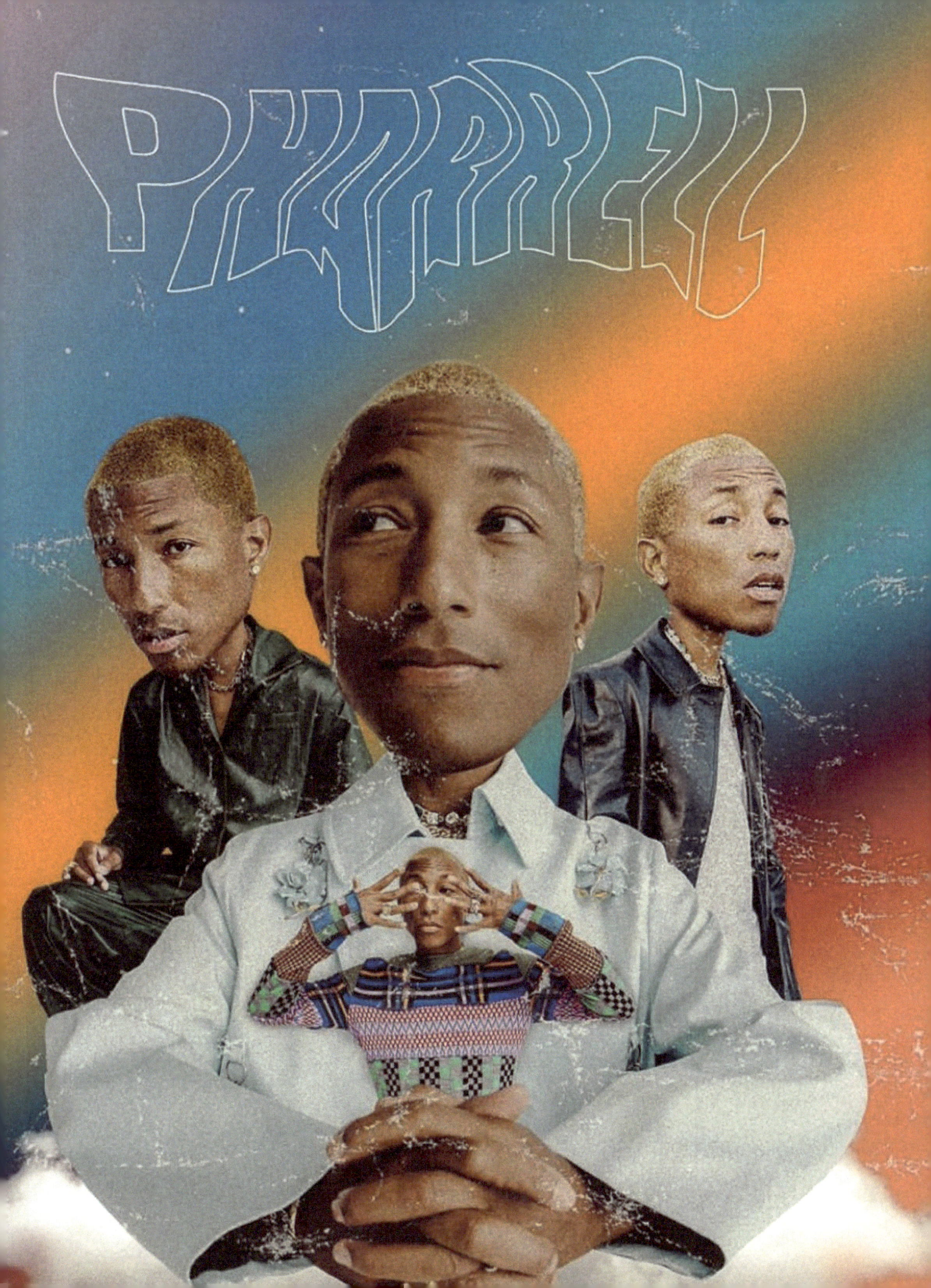

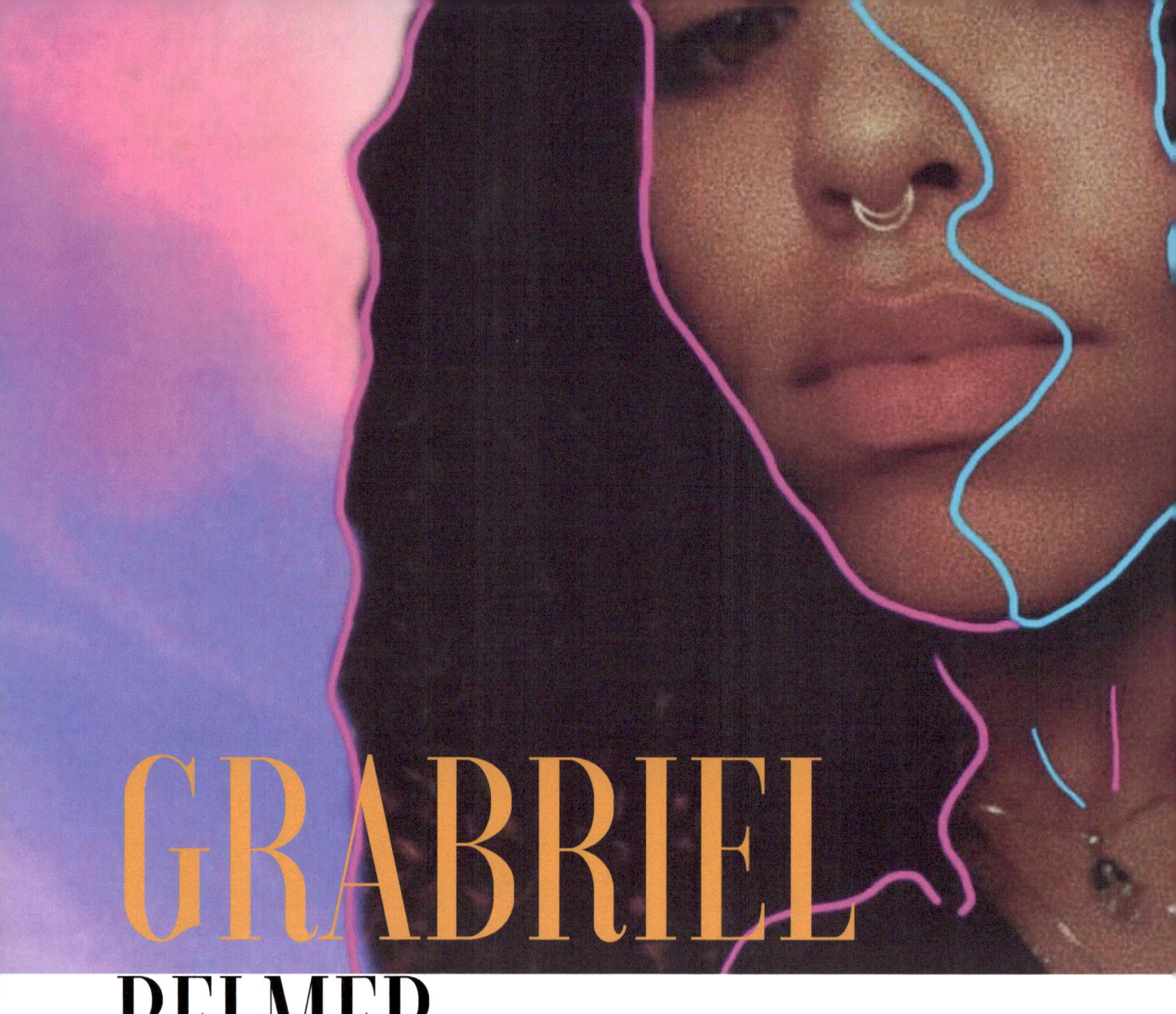

GRABRIEL BELMER

Being able to experiment with art at a young age truly has it benefits, and Gabrielle can attest to this. As a child her nana would always take her to art museums and they'd constantly do crafts, and it really shows in her artwork. With her goal wanted to be in an art museum, she definitely believes that she's following the right path.

Gabrielle also proves how art can be used to express your emotions. While she was in a low state of mind, she used that time to push her creativity to its upmost limit.

She stated, "I'm extremely grateful for me feeling down at the time because I found something I was passionate about."

"I HOPE TO REACH PLACES I NEVER THOUGHT WERE POSSIBLE!"

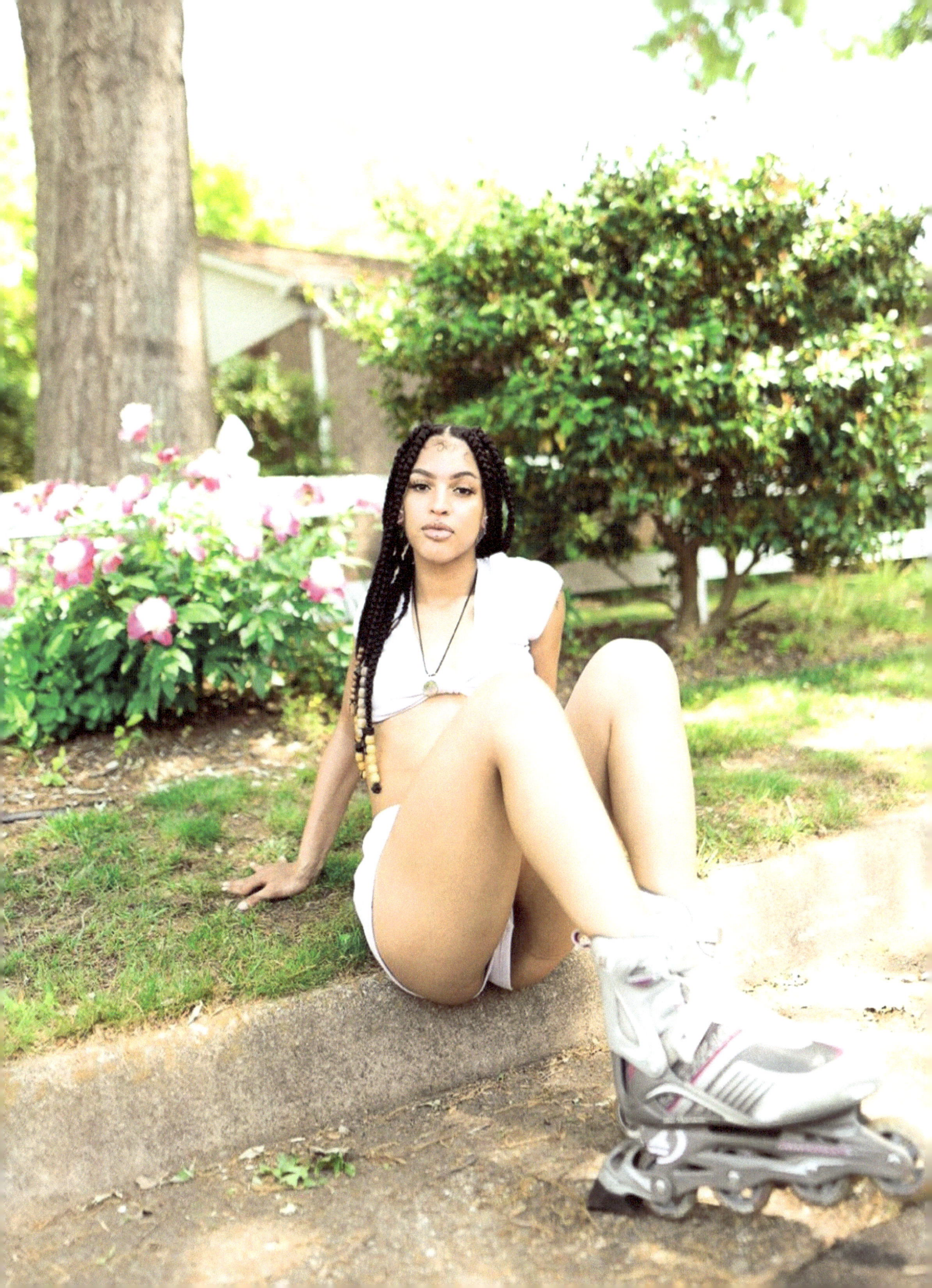

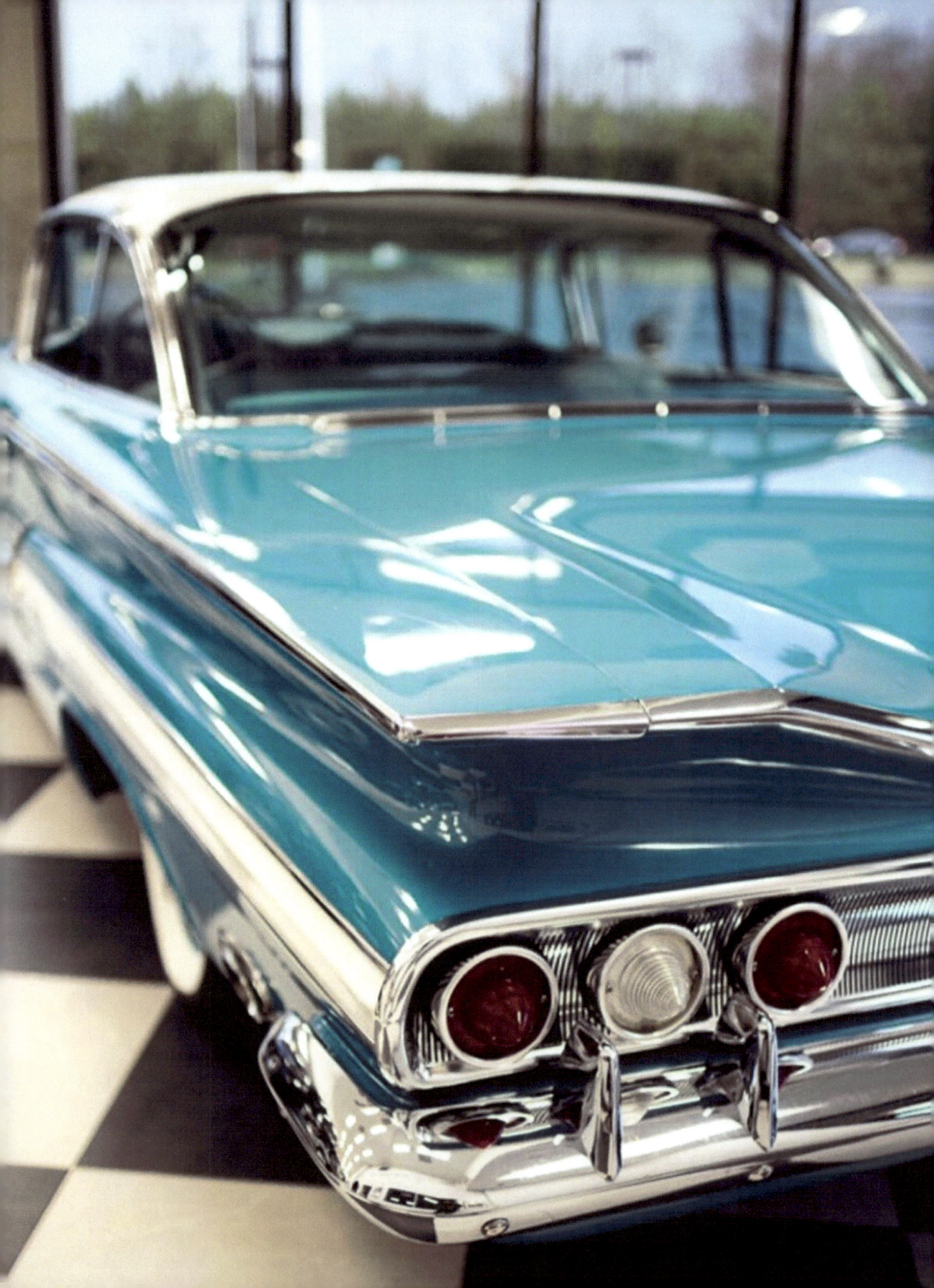

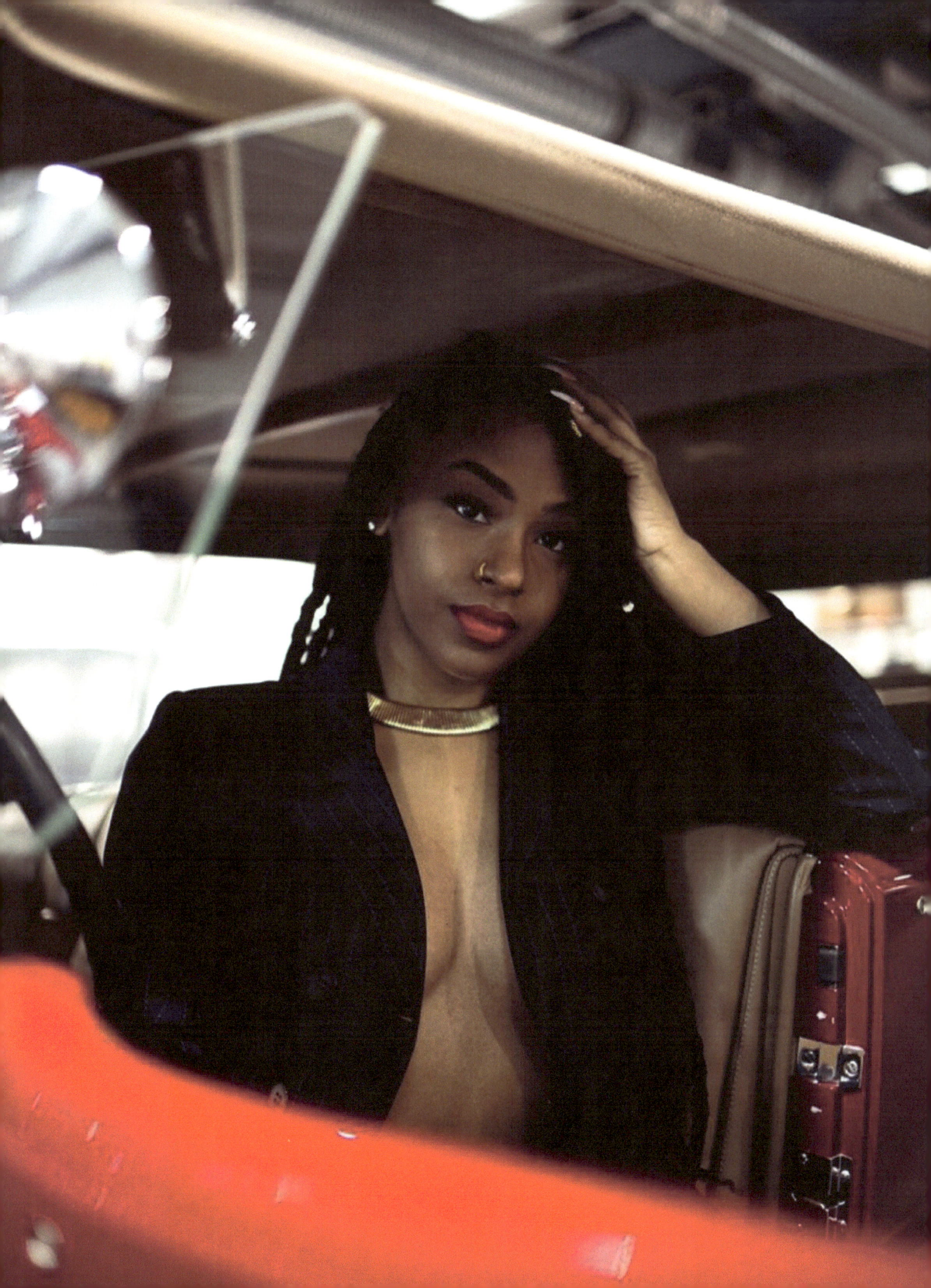

Daiquan Davis
Photographer

Inspired by life and the people around him, Daiquan started photography after he graduated high school. For the past 5 years, he's been proving himself to be a master behind the camera. With each of his shoots containing different elements of style and artistry, he pulls out the full potential of his models and captures pictures of a lifetime. His photographs have such warm essence to them you'll have no choice but to support his craftsmanship. Although, he starting photography by capturing the sunrise in the morning, you can see how much he developed his work.

"Daiquan's work is undeniably good! His eye for detail is immaculate, and he's the most down to earth photographer I have ever worked with! " ~ Natural Glover

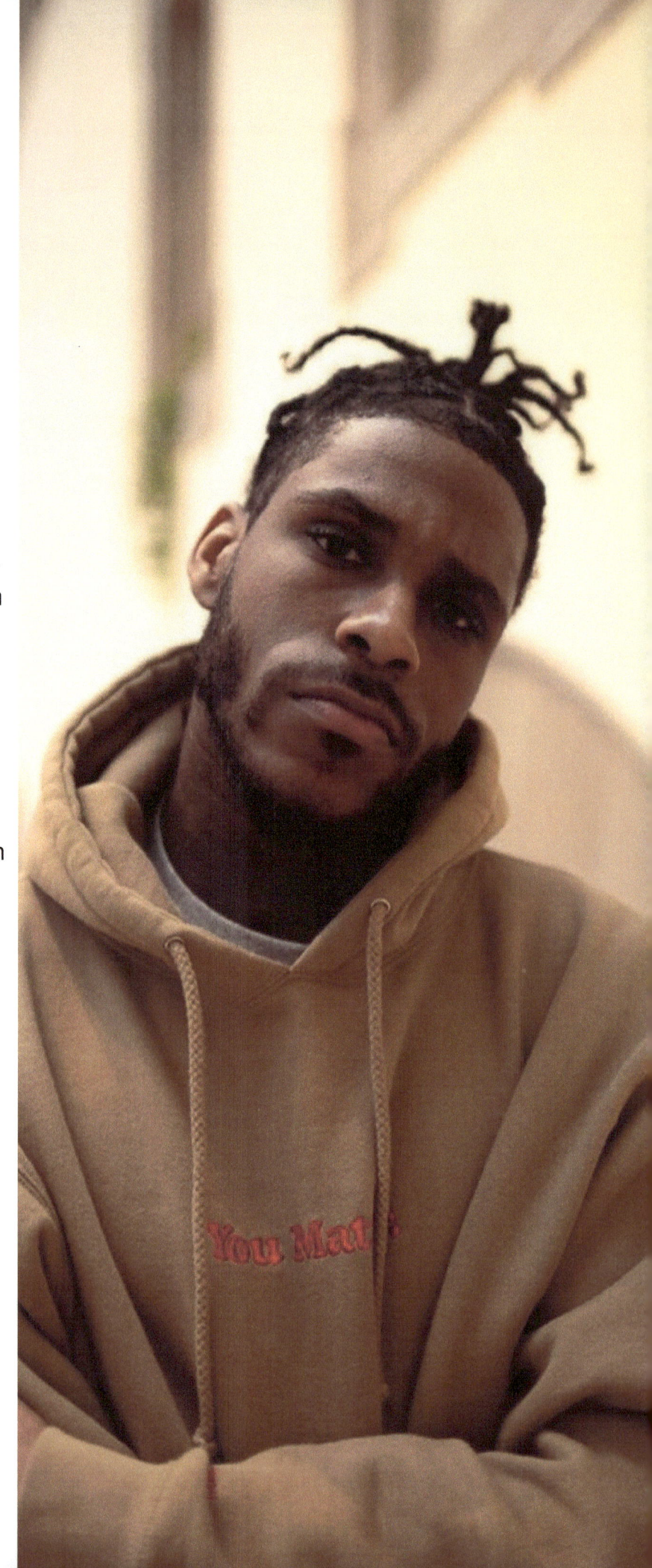

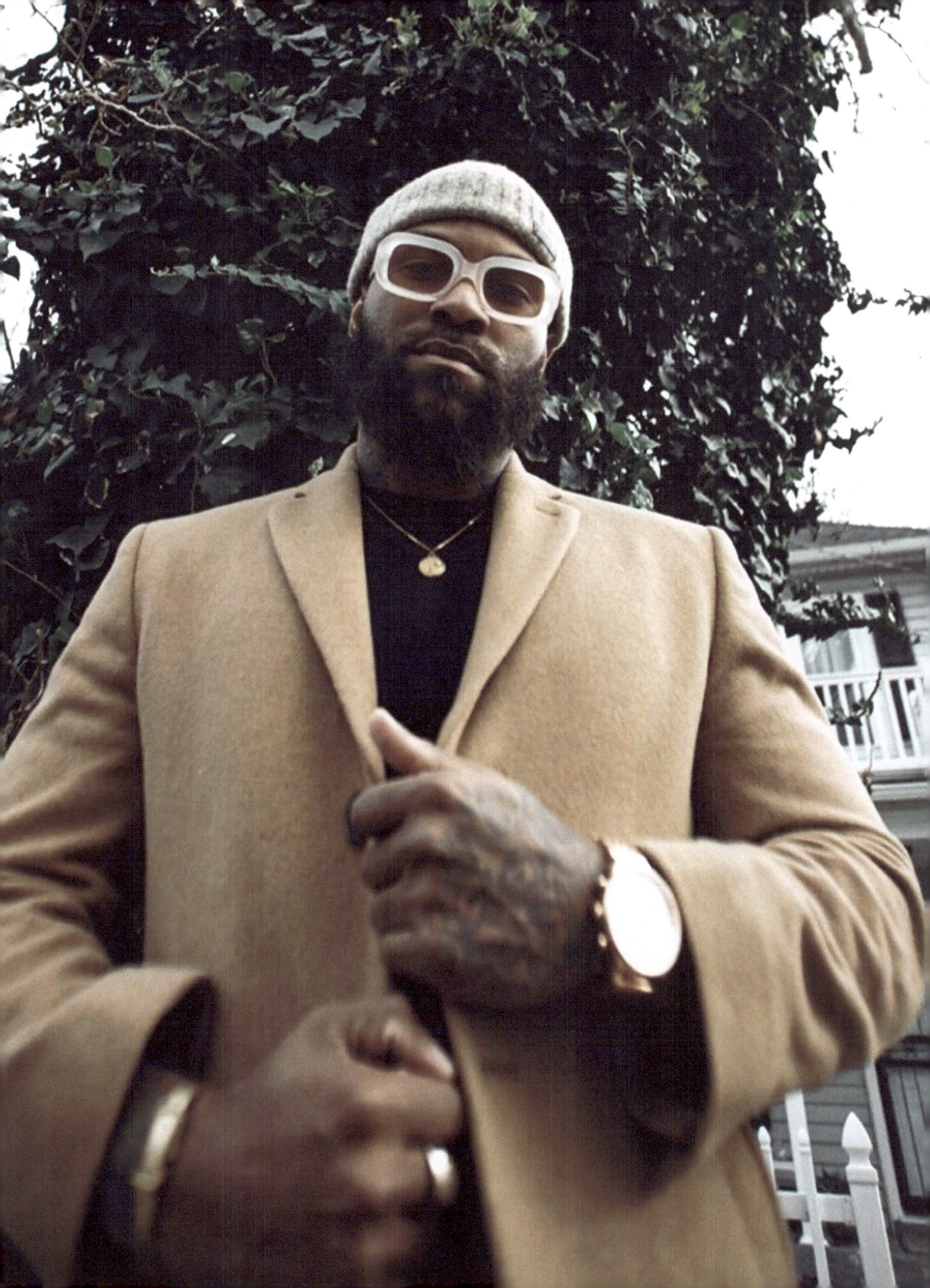

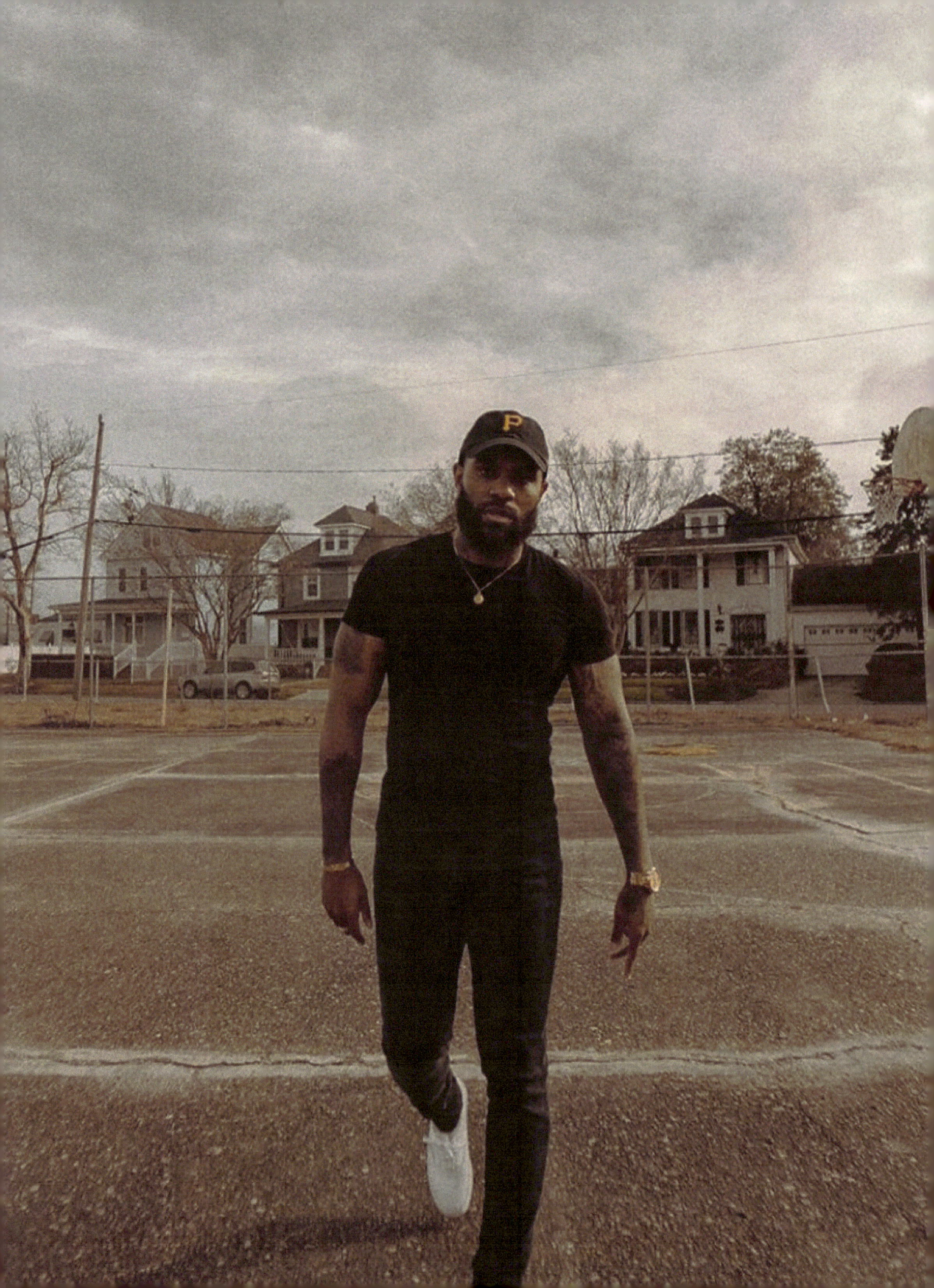

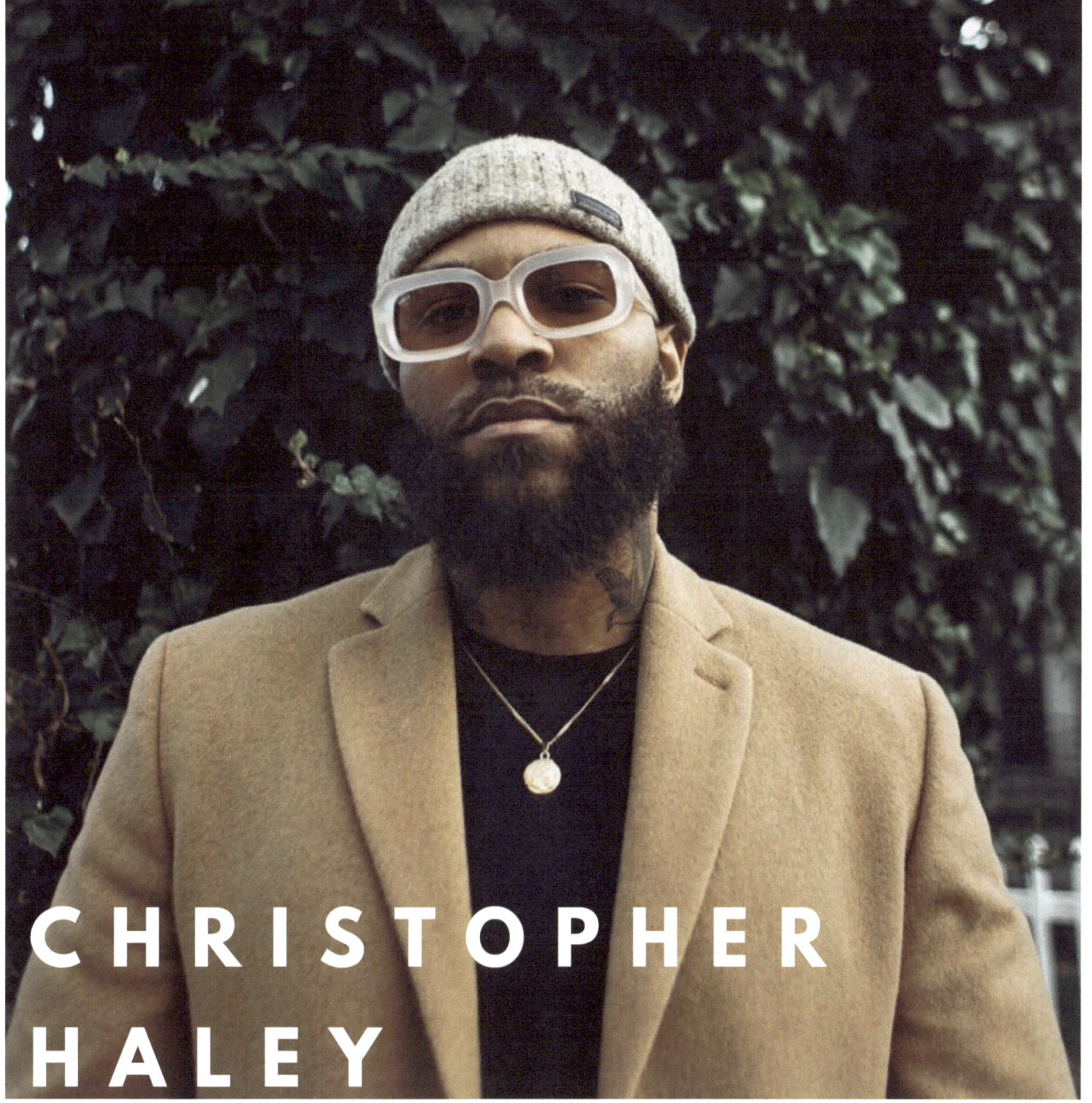

CHRISTOPHER HALEY

Christopher is a true man of class, and you can tell by his modeling. His portfolio is one to be amazed by, working with photographers such as Christian Dillard. He combines his sense of fashion and mixes it with his confidence, which brings out the best in him. You can see the pride & poise within each shot he takes. When asked where can modeling take him, Chris stated, "I see it as a vehicle to tap into other markets like acting or getting involved in other different platforms." Chris's favorite motto is "Chase your dreams," and right now, he's beyond doubt doing that.

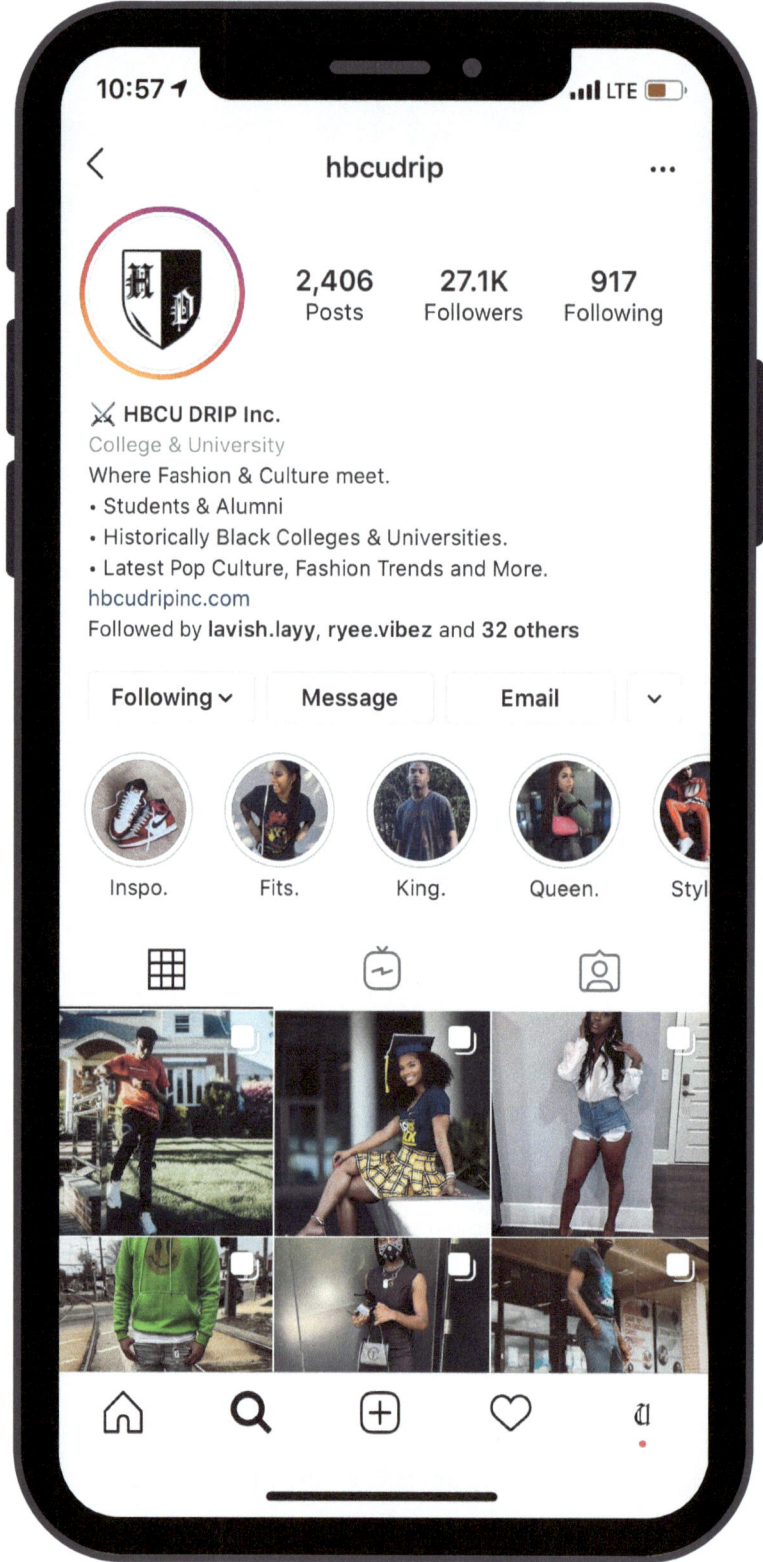

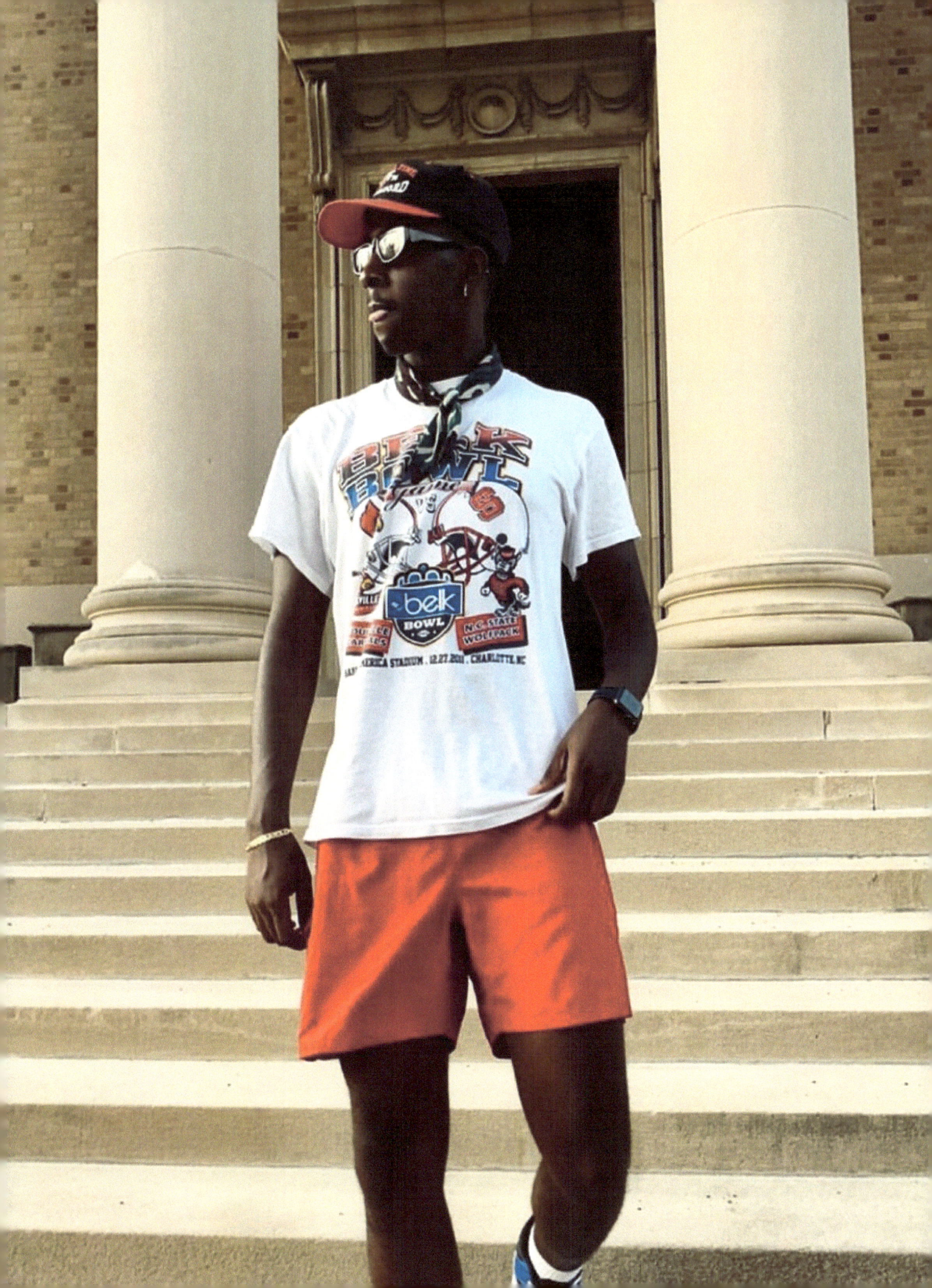

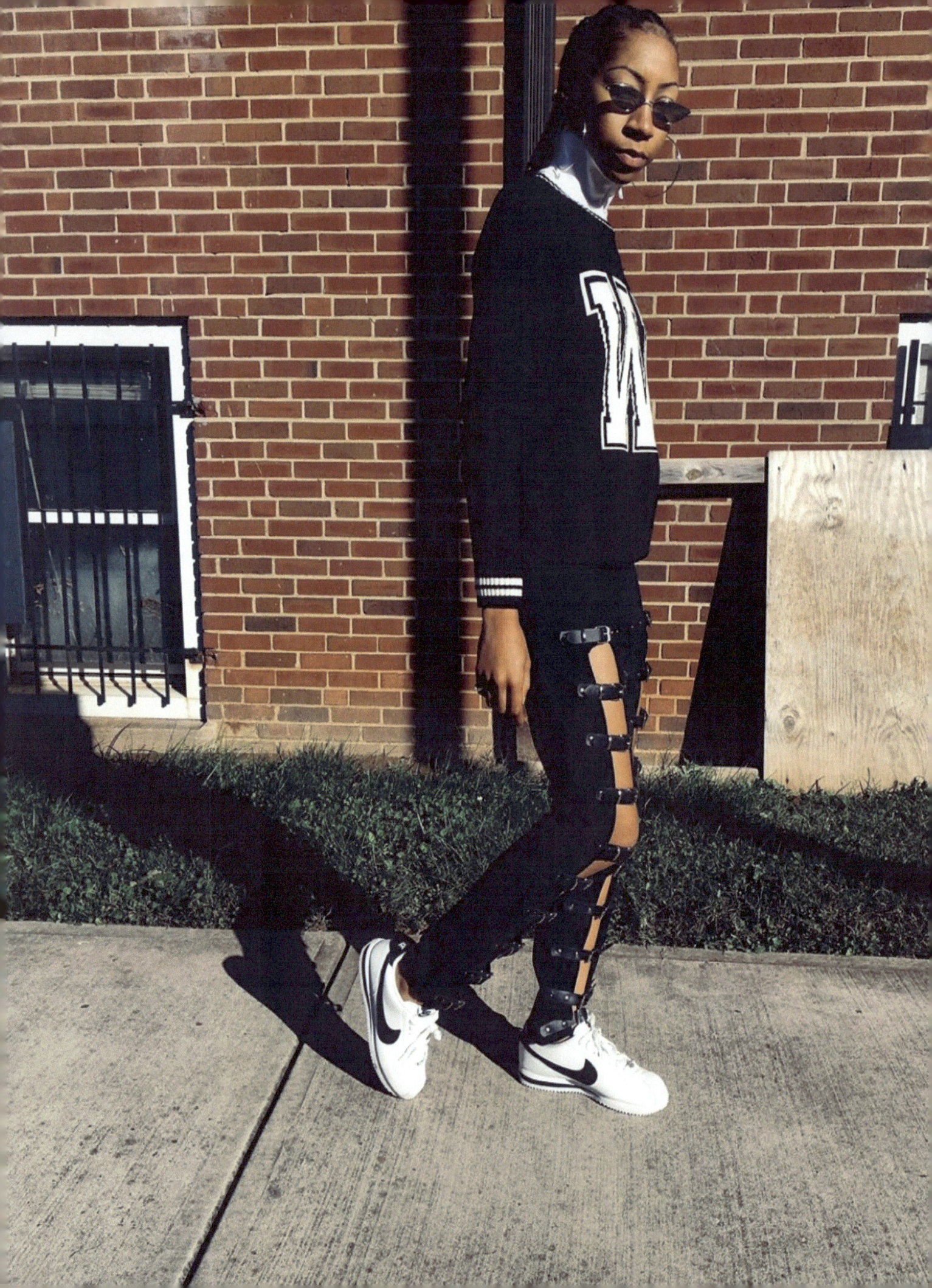

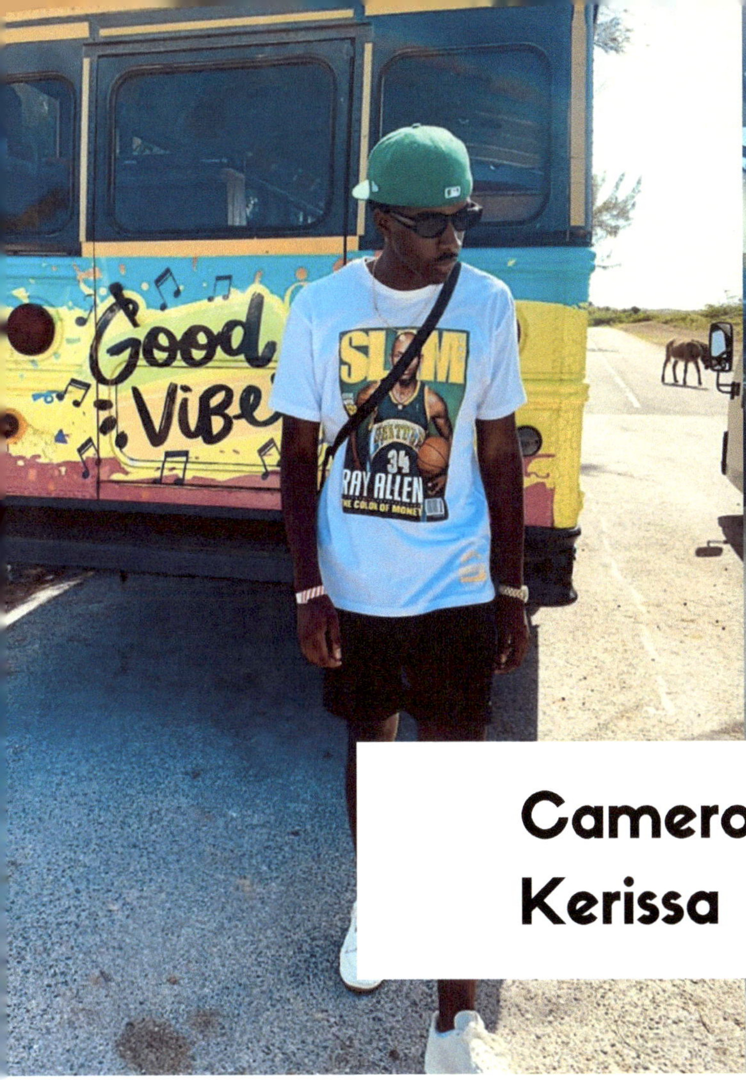

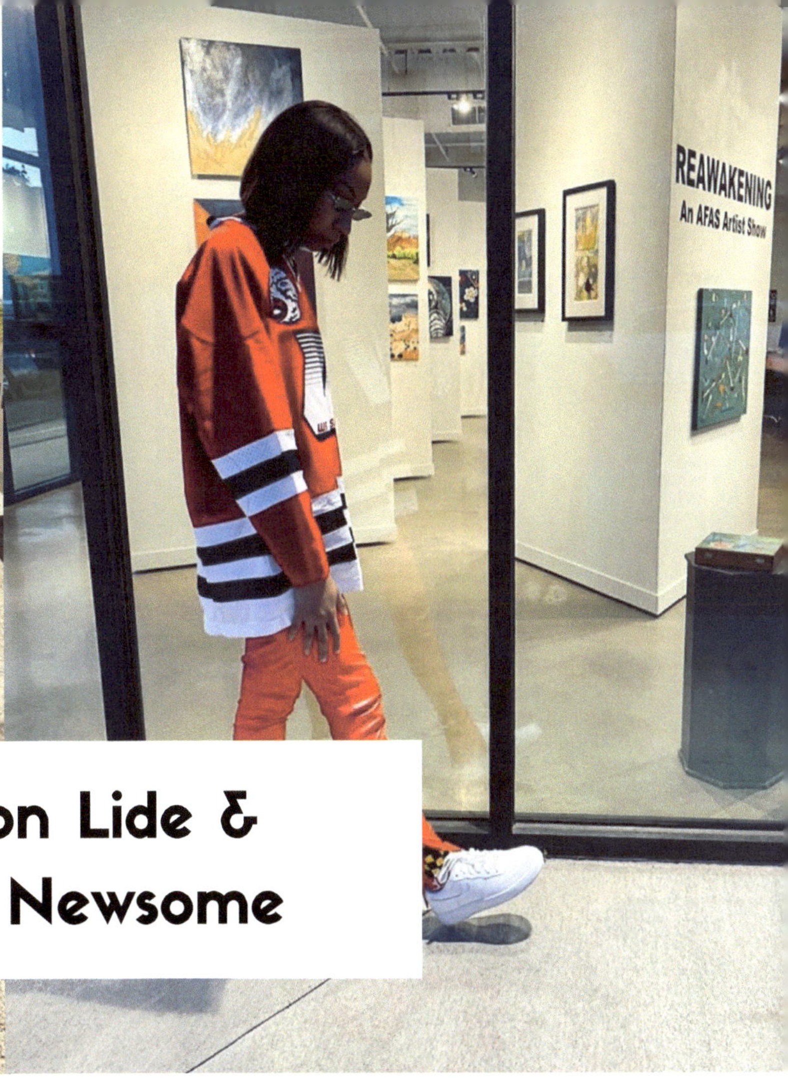

Cameron Lide & Kerissa Newsome

Cameron and Kerissa, creators of famous Instagram page "@hbcudrip," has their eyes set to the stars when it comes to the platform they created. The inspiration for the page came from @leaguefits on Instagram, and how professional athletes got to show off their pregame outfits. They felt like there needed to be a platform that could be the epicenter for black fashion, so they dug to the root of it all; H.B.C. U's. After only being active for a year they've reached over 26k followers and plans to take it even further than just social media, by eventually creating jobs for future H.B.C.U. graduates who love being involved in fashion and pop culture.

> " Cam & I had no idea how popular the page would become in just a matter of months."
>
> KERISSA NEWSOME

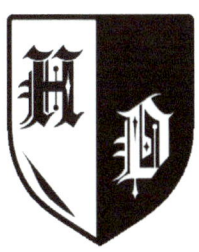

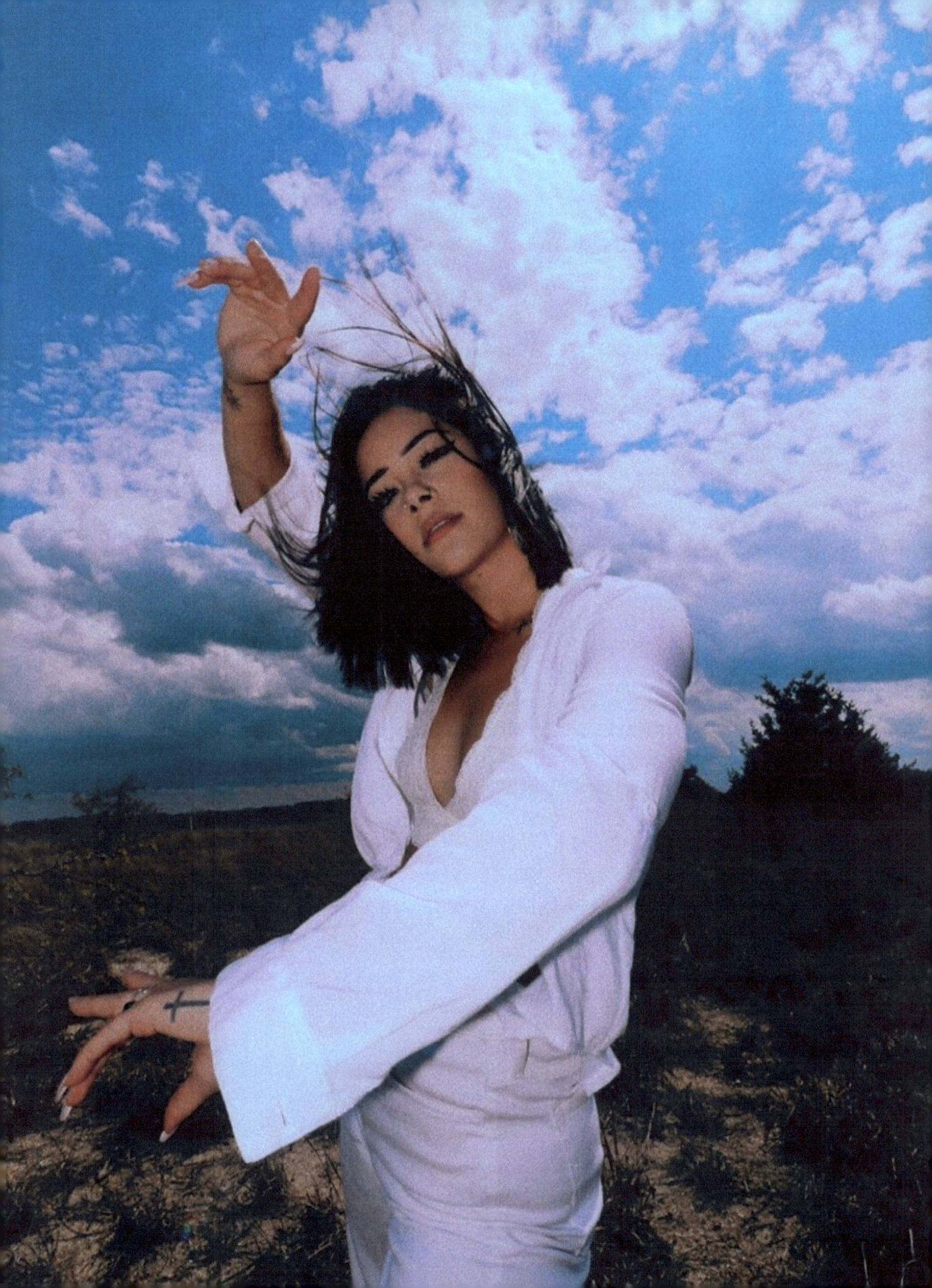

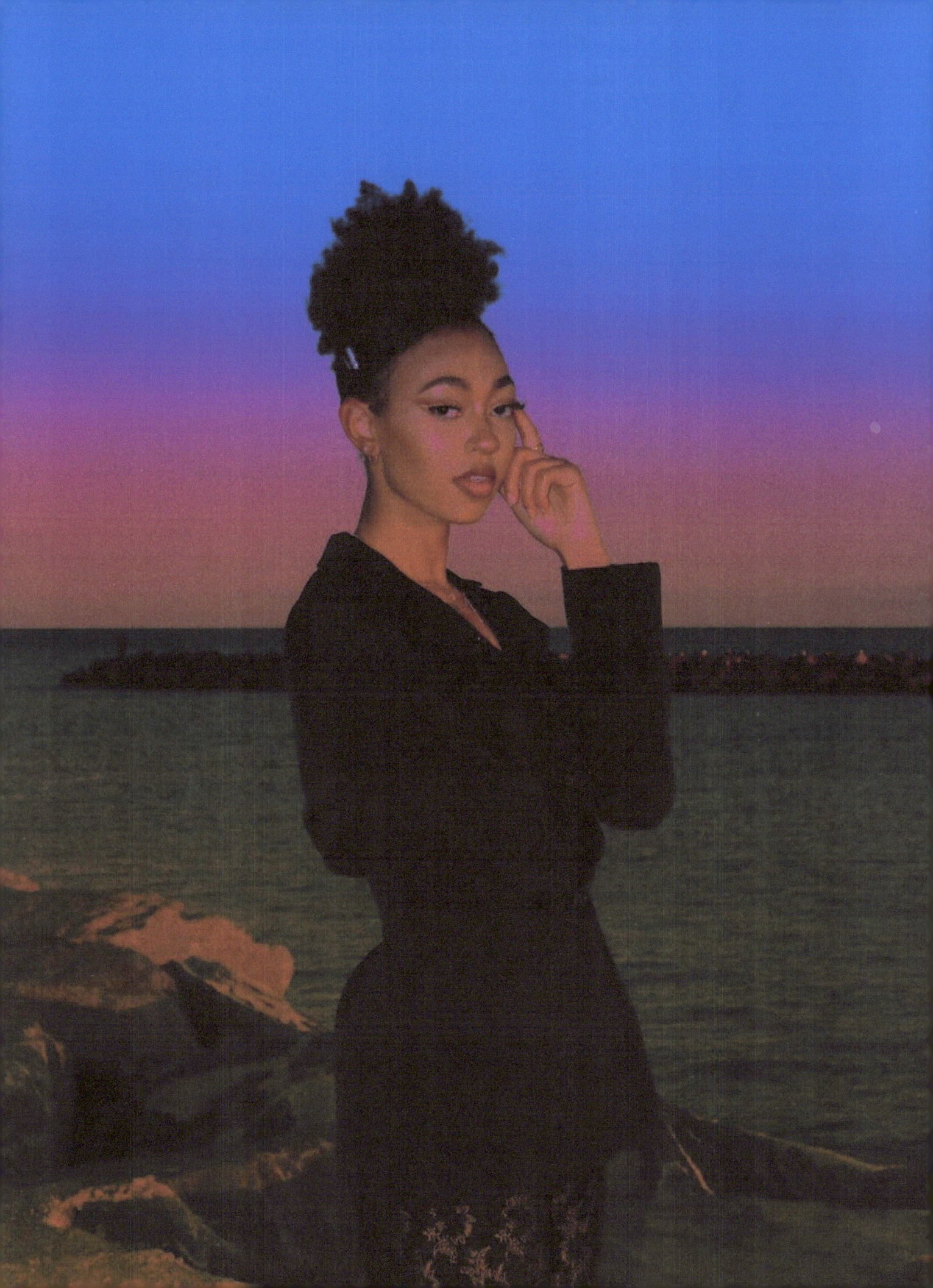

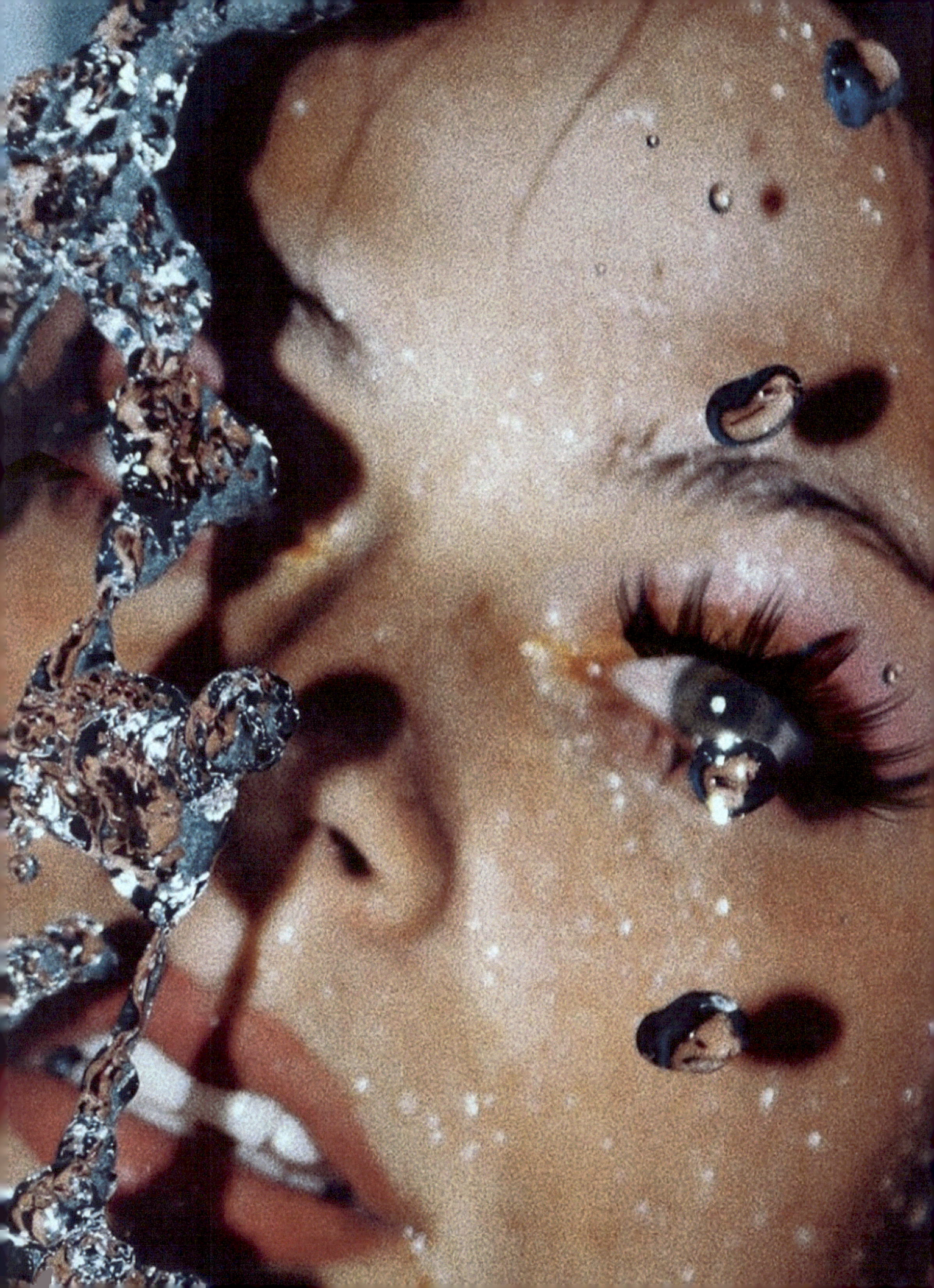

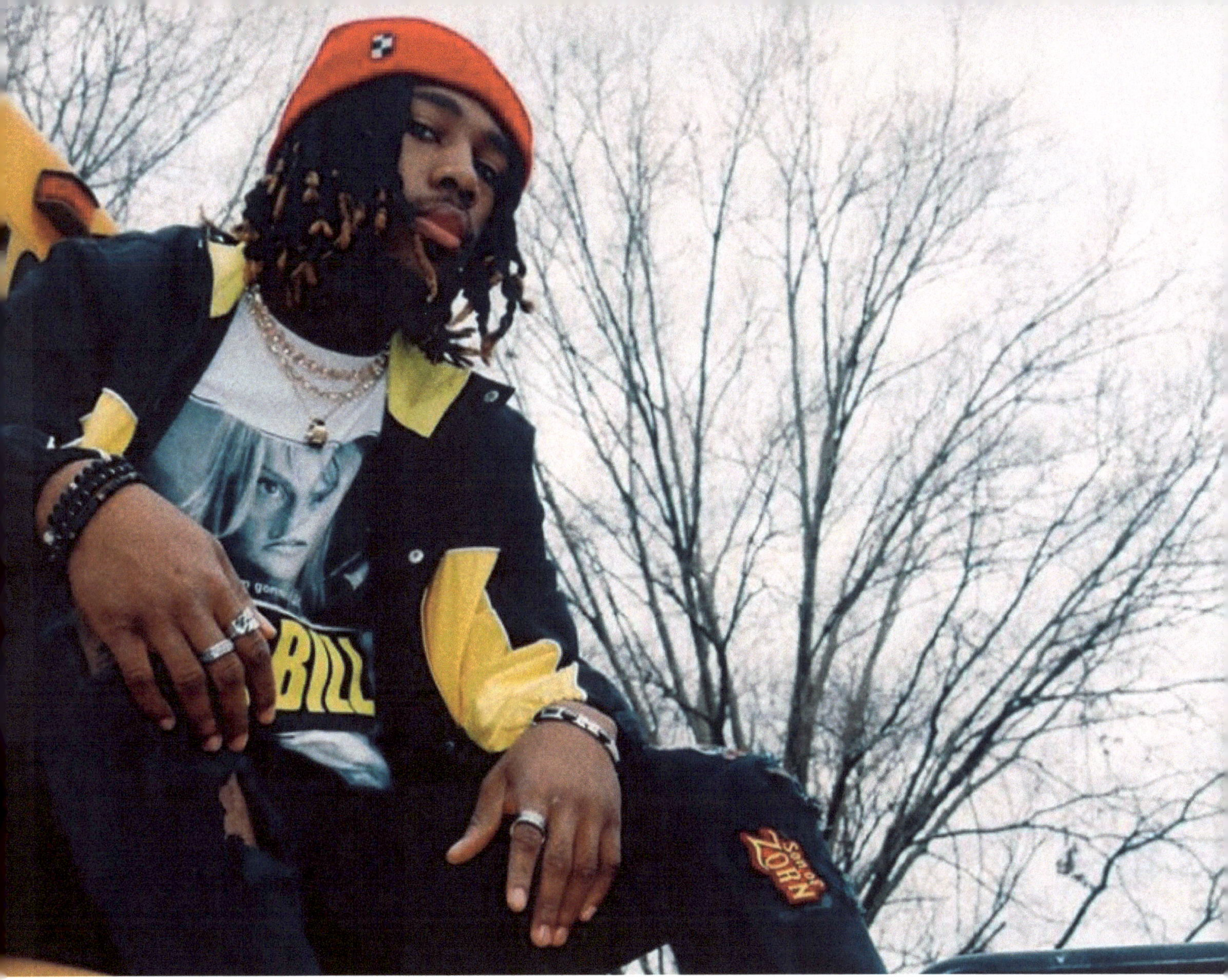

Jordan Pope

PHOTOGRAPHER

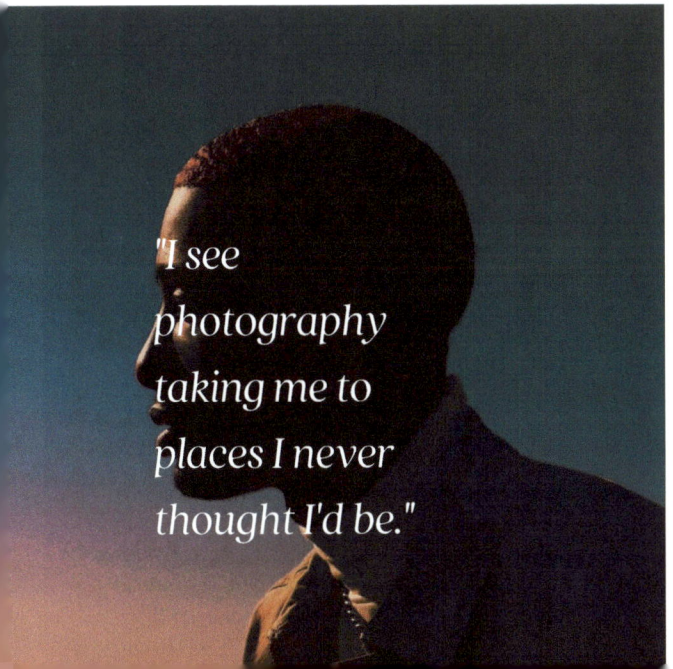

"I see photography taking me to places I never thought I'd be."

If it wasn't for his friends pushing him to pursue photography, Jordan would've never realized how talented he truly is. People say that there's no such thing as natural talent, but Jordan would beg to differ. The way he portrays each photograph with so much emotion, there's a reason why he has one of the best portfolio's to date. He unearths inspiration from the world, from music, to colors, to fashion, and no matter what it is, he'll try to find a deeper meaning and convert it into a masterpiece.

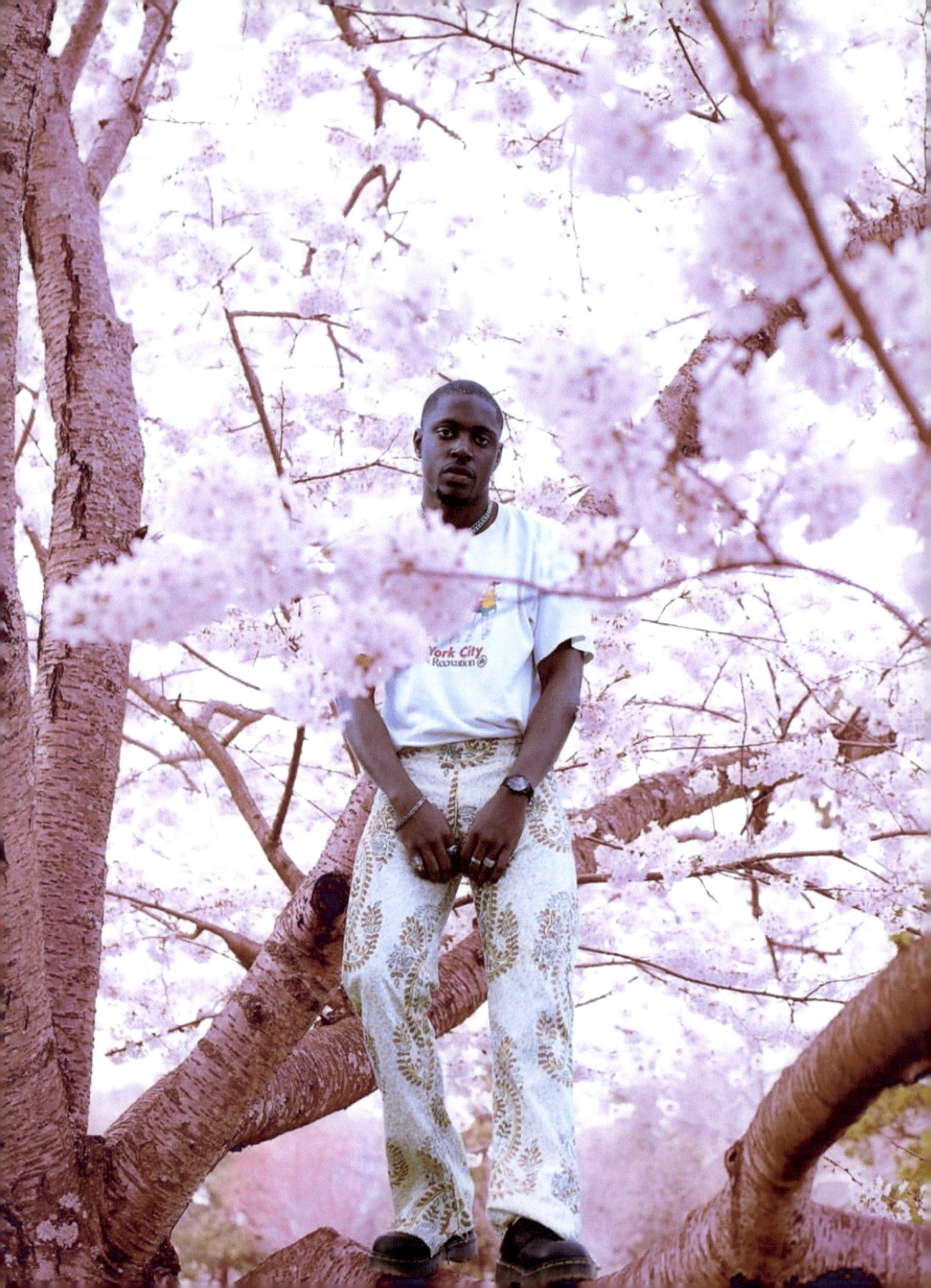

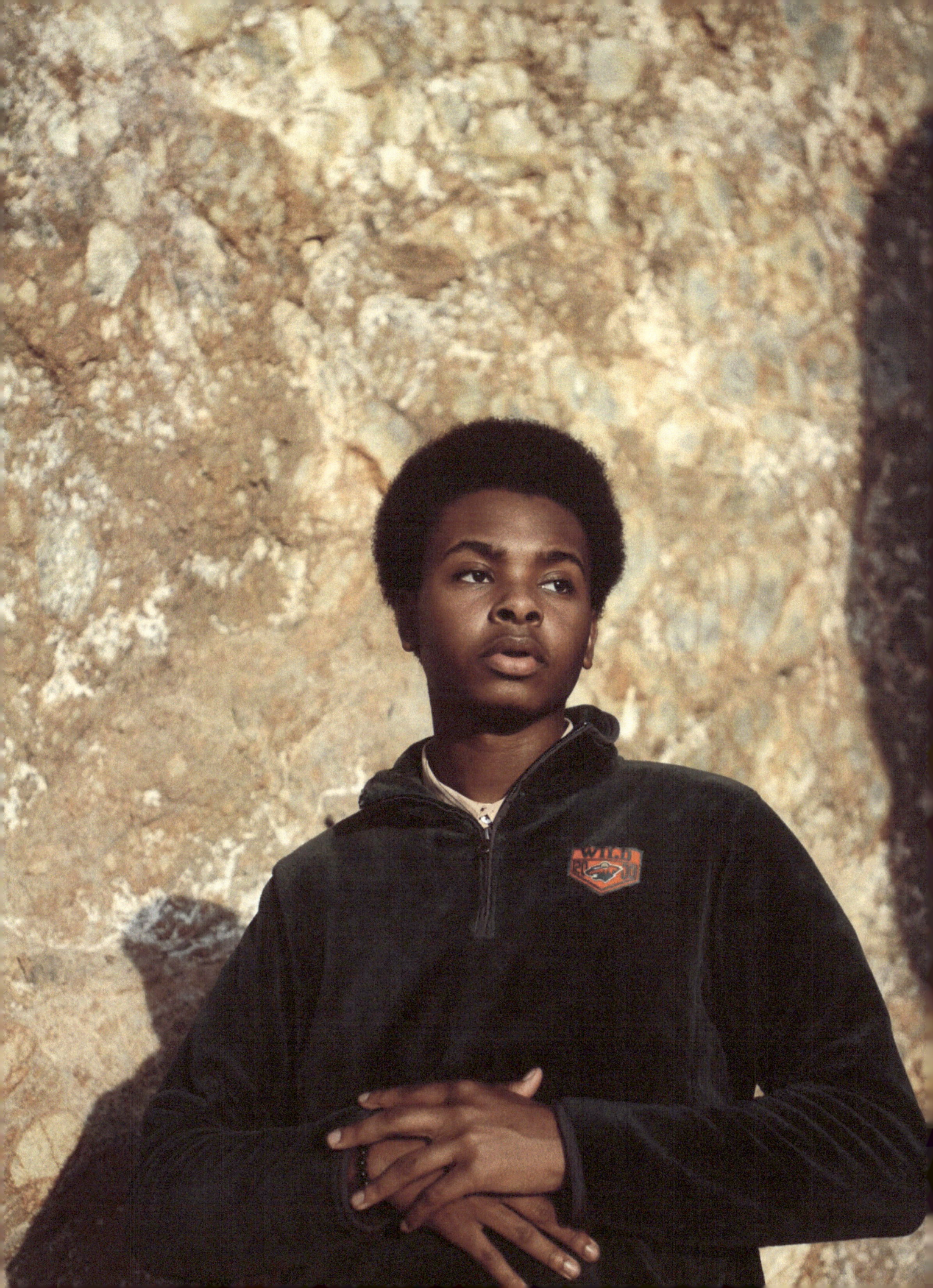

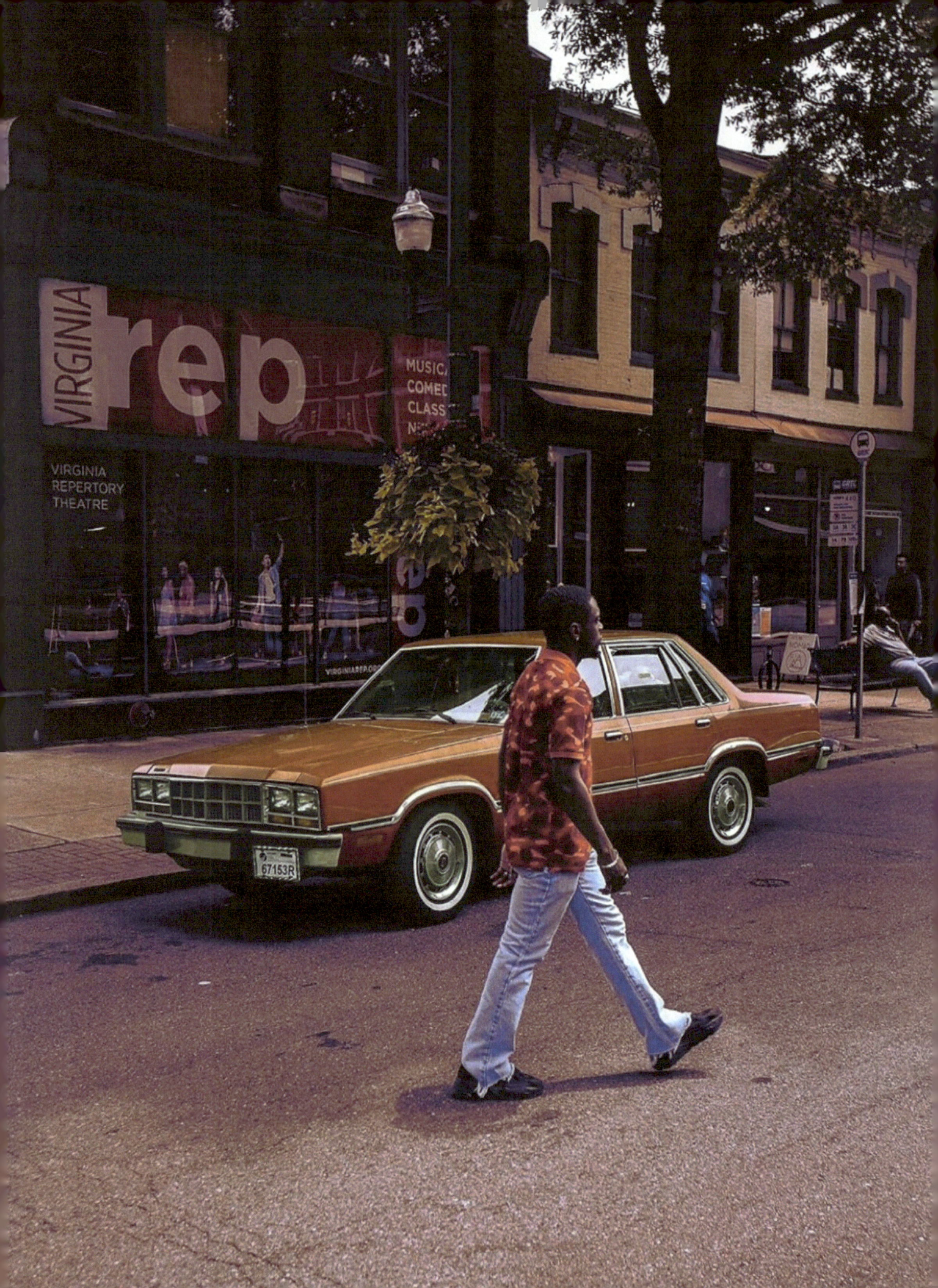

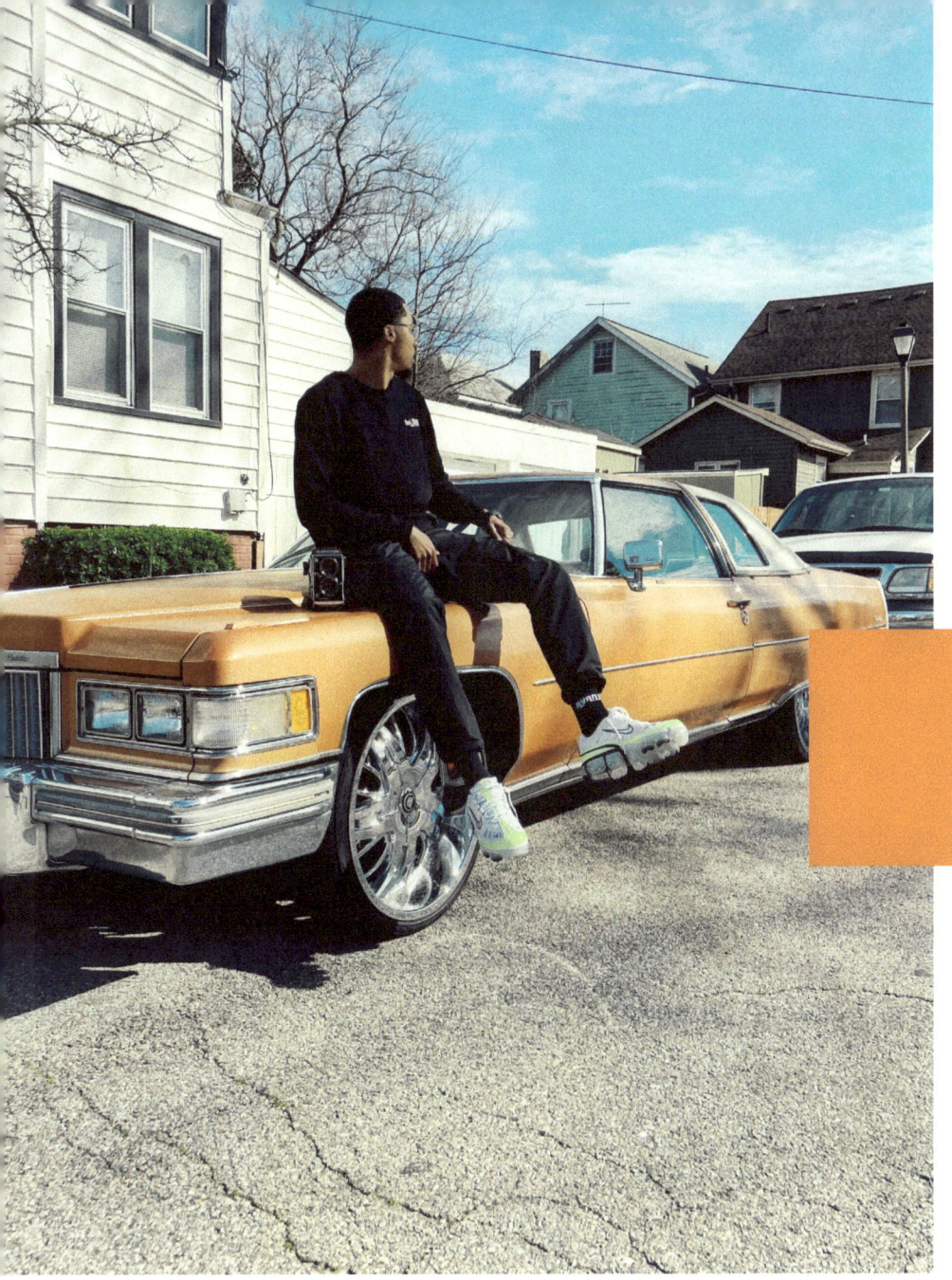

"30"
Renowned Photographer

One of the most stimulating photographers in Virginia, 30, has truly made a name for himself throughout the years. The rush he gets when shooting is always at the max, whether it's a model, artist, or a car. When asked what inspires him, he stated, "My friends inspire me, I surround myself with like minded individuals that have a real drive for what they do." Subsequently, everyone he's surrounded himself with, has some form of success in their lives, no matter how big or small. However, being enveloped with such individuals is pushing 30 to evolve his own craftsmanship.

In short, we asked 30 if he had any words of inspiration for aspiring photographers, he expressed, "Don't shoot with everybody. You must figure out who you are as a shooter and what you want to shoot, stamp it and pave your own lane, learn the fundamentals."

"We all start somewhere so when you go to a photographers page and you might feel as if their work is better than yours, you've lost."

Stay Safe during this pandemic.